Wuthering Heights

by Emily Brontë
A post–16 study guide

written and devised by Christine Hall and Mary Bailey

Series editor: Sue Dymoke

NATE

The *Critical Reading* series is published jointly by the National Association for the Teaching of English (NATE), the UK subject teacher association for all aspects of the teaching of English from pre-school to university, and York Publishing Servicers Ltd.

NATE
50 Broadfield Road
Sheffield S8 0XJ

Tel: 0114 255 5419
Fax: 0114 255 5296
E-mail: nate.hq@campus.bt.com

All page references within this book are to the Penguin Classics 1995 edition of *Wuthering Heights*.

British Library Cataloguing in Publication data. A catalogue record for this book is available from the British Library.

ISBN 0 901291 58 7

Printed in the United Kingdom by York Publishing Services Ltd, 64 Hallfield Road, Layerthorpe, York YO3 7XQ

Contents

Acknowledgements

We are grateful to the following for permission to reproduce illustrations:
The Ronald Grant Archive, pages 2 and 3; © The Bronte Society, pages 5, 7 and
11; Simon Warner, page 6; The National Portrait Gallery, pages 8 and 9.

We are grateful to the following for permission to reproduce text:
Lyrics from *Wuthering Heights*, Kate Bush/EMI; *Myths of Power,* Terry Eagleton
published by Macmillan Ltd.

Before reading

Representations of *Wuthering Heights*

> The twentieth century has seen an enormous advance in both the popularity and the critical esteem enjoyed by Emily Brontë's novel. Indeed, *Wuthering Heights* is one of those rare texts which has transcended its literary origin to become part of the lexicon of popular culture – the subject of film, song and even comedy.
> (Nestor, 1995)

■ Discuss what you already knew about *Wuthering Heights* before reading it: the story, characters, settings, mood, images, associations.

■ Where does this knowledge come from? Can you think of any particular ways in which you have 'heard the story' before?

Look at the images and extracts on this and the following page. For each of them consider:

■ what aspect of *Wuthering Heights* is emphasised in this image or extract?

■ how close do you feel this might be to the original *Wuthering Heights?*

■ what is your response to it?

1978 Kate Bush song – No. 1 in the BBC Top 40 for four weeks

Out on the wiley, windy moors
We'd roll and fall in green.
You had a temper like my jealousy:
Too hot, too greedy.
How could you leave me,
When I needed to possess you?
I hated you. I loved you, too.

Bad dreams in the night.
They told me I was going to lose the fight,
Leave behind my wuthering, wuthering
Wuthering Heights.

(Chorus)
Heathcliff, it's me – Cathy.
Come home. I'm so cold!
Let me in-a-your window.
Heathcliff, it's me – Cathy.
Come home. I'm so cold!
Let me in-a-your window.

Ooh, it gets dark! It gets lonely,
On the other side from you.
I pine a lot. I find the lot
Falls through without you.
I'm coming back, love.
Cruel Heathcliff, my one dream,
My only master.

Too long I roam in the night.
I'm coming back to his side, to put it right.
I'm coming home to wuthering, wuthering,
Wuthering Heights,
(Chorus)

Ooh! Let me have it.
Let me grab your soul away.
Ooh! Let me have it.
Let me grab your soul away.
You know it's me – Cathy!
(Chorus)

1939 *Wuthering Heights* film (Director: William Wyler)

Starring Laurence Olivier as Heathcliff and Merle Oberon as Cathy, this was the first talking film dramatisation of the novel, concentrating on the first two-thirds of the book. A synopsis of this film version begins in this way:

> The credits play over views of Wuthering Heights, an estate on the edge of the storm-tossed Yorkshire Moors.
>
> On the barren Yorkshire Moors in England, a hundred years ago, stood a house as bleak and desolate as the wastes around it. Only a stranger lost in a storm would have dared to knock at the door of Wuthering Heights.
>
> During a raging blizzard, a bitterly cold, snowy night on the moors, a solitary traveller staggers for refuge toward Wuthering Heights. In the dark, mysterious house, Mr. Lockwood, a 'new tenant at the Grange,' announces to his landlord Heathcliff and his wife Isabella that he is lost and must stay the night for shelter. Although given a cold reception, Lockwood is grudgingly given a room. He is led by candlelight to a drafty, depressing, upstairs 'bridal chamber' guest room by Joseph, where he is told: 'Nobody slept here for years.'
>
> (from the Filmsite web site – http://www.filmsite.org/wuth.html)

1992 *Wuthering Heights* film (Director: Peter Kosminsky, Paramount)

Starring Juliette Binoche as Cathy and Ralph Fiennes as Heathcliff.

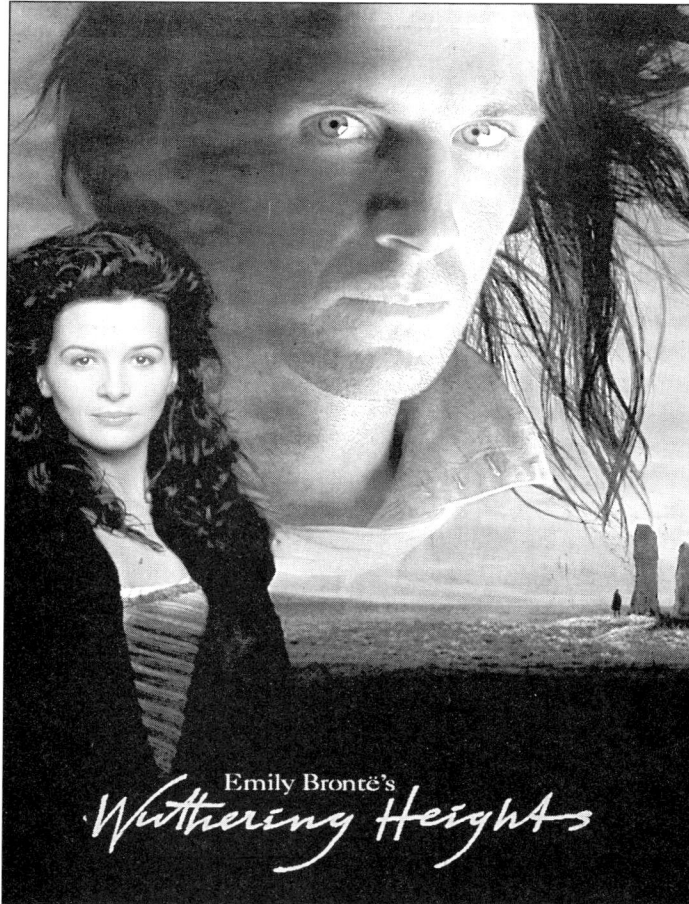

Emily Brontë's *Wuthering Heights*

1994 *Heathcliff,* the musical

Starring Cliff Richard, *Heathcliff* toured the UK from November 1994 to May 1997.

Cliff Aims to be a Brooder

Cliff Richard surveys the bleak beauty of the moors as he draws inspiration for the most demanding role of his life. The nice guy of pop is determined to create a convincing portrayal of the cruel and brooding Heathcliff of Emily Brontë's *Wuthering Heights.* As he paused on the steep road above the desolate countryside surrounding Emily's birthplace in Haworth, West Yorkshire, Richard contemplated the solitude. It didn't last long. The singer was being shadowed by two film crews, two press photographers and a personal assistant ... Cynics have scoffed at the idea of a warm-hearted self-confessed celibate playing Heathcliff ... The musical, which will blend pop and theatre and feature projections of Haworth Moor behind a 30-metre stage, opens in November.

(*The Herald Sun,* 23 March 1994)

1994 Titles of songs from *Heathcliff*, an album by Cliff Richard, lyrics by Sir Tim Rice and music by John Farrar

Misunderstood Man	Dream Tomorrow
Sleep of the Good	I Do Not Love You Isabella
Gypsy Bundle	Choosing When It's Too Late
Had To Be	Marked With Death
When You Thought of Me	Be With Me Always

Can you think of any other examples of popular representations of *Wuthering Heights* or references to it that you have seen or heard, for example in television comedy sketches?

When you know *Wuthering Heights* more thoroughly you might like to look at these extracts again and note whether your view of them is any different.

Haworth today

The village of Haworth, with the parsonage which was the home of the Brontë family, has become a popular tourist site. The Brontë Parsonage Museum, managed by the Brontë Society, is open for most of the year and receives around 100,000 visitors annually. In addition to the museum, and its collection of what is affectionately known as 'Bronteana', there is a shop selling books, educational materials and gifts, as well as a programme of educational courses. The surrounding countryside is marketed by the Yorkshire Tourist Board as 'Brontë Country'.

Read the following extracts from publicity material published by the Brontë Parsonage Museum and the Yorkshire Tourist Board.

- How are the Brontës presented in this material?

- How are their works presented?

- How are Haworth and other places presented?

- How are the two extracts different, in the above respects and in the use of language, the tone and the implied audience?

- When you have read the extracts, consider the meaning of the following statement in relation to the representations of Haworth and Brontë Country:

> The Brontë name has become inseparably linked with that of Haworth ... It is often assumed that the Yorkshire moors stand in a similar relation to the Brontë novels as the lakes and hills of Cumbria do to the poetry of Wordsworth. But that is the trouble: Haworth has become virtually synonymous with a *natural* landscape ... There is no doubt that *Wuthering Heights* is in crucial ways a response to a given environment, but that environment is not composed entirely of stunted trees, rocks, furze and unyielding winds.
> (Mengham, 1988, page 17)

The Brontë Parsonage Museum

The Brontës were an extraordinary literary family and Haworth Parsonage was their lifelong home. The Reverend Patrick Brontë, his wife Maria and their six children came to live at the parsonage in 1820. Maria and Elizabeth, the eldest girls, died here in childhood, not long after their mother. Charlotte, Branwell, Emily and Anne survived into adulthood, the sisters to write some of the greatest novels in the English language: Charlotte's *Jane Eyre*, 1847, Emily's *Wuthering Heights*, 1847, and Anne's *The Tenant of Wildfell Hall*, 1848.

The Brontës were an intensely close-knit family and their parsonage home formed the heart of their world from early childhood until the ends of their brief lives. The Yorkshire moorland setting provided them with inspiration for their writing.

Much of the Museum's collection is on show: the furniture Charlotte bought with the proceeds of her literary success, her dress, bonnet and tiny shoes; the Brontë children's earliest literary efforts, their hand-made 'little books'; Branwell's portraits of local worthies; Emily's writing desk, with its contents as she left them; Anne's books and drawings, even the pebbles she collected on the beach at Scarborough, the place where she died and is buried.

The Brontë Society was founded in 1893 to cherish and foster what is now a world-wide interest in the Brontës' outstanding literary achievements. The Society cares for the Brontes' home, which opened as a museum in 1928, and the magnificent collections of books, manuscripts, paintings and personal memorabilia which it contains. The parsonage rooms have as far as possible been restored to their appearance in the early 1850s ...

(from a Brontë Parsonage Museum leaflet)

Haworth Parsonage today

Top Withins

Brontë Country

Welcome to Brontë Country, an area of Pennine upland in West Yorkshire, England. A windswept land of heather and wild moors, it is hardly surprising that this area became the inspiration for the classic works of the Brontë sisters, Charlotte, Emily and Anne.

Geographically, Brontë Country consists of the Pennine hills immediately to the west of the Bradford/Leeds West Yorkshire conurbation. Unlike the pastoral limestone valleys of the Yorkshire Dales further north, the geology in Brontë Country is predominantly of Millstone Grit, a dark sandstone which lends the crags and scenery here an air of bleakness and desolation. Small wonder then, that this landscape fuelled the imagination of the Brontës' writings in classics such as *Wuthering Heights* (which was reputably inspired by the isolated moorland farm of Top Withins) ...

Although at odds with her description in the novel *Wuthering Heights*, Top Withins is popularly credited as being Emily Brontë's setting for Heathcliff's moorland farmstead. Whether or not this desolate ruin on the moors above Haworth is the genuine article hardly seems to matter to most visitors; the setting is romantic enough to have appeared in several film versions and, even on a fine day, it is hard not to be impressed by the wildness of the place. Well worth a visit – for Bronte enthusiasts and philistines alike ...

Many public footpaths lead out of the village [of Haworth], and there is much scope for rambling, though perhaps the most famous walk leads past Stanbury Reservoir to the picturesque (but unspectacular) Brontë Falls, the Brontë Bridge, and the Brontë Stone Chair in which (it is said) the sisters took turns to sit and write their first stories. This path (which forms part of the 64 km (40 mile) long Brontë Way) then leads out of the valley and up on the moors...

(from the Yorkshire Tourist Board's Brontë Country web site, Nov. 1997 – http://www.eagle.co.uk/Bronte)

The Brontë family: biographical information

- Patrick Brontë, Emily's father was born in 1777 in Northern Ireland. After attending Cambridge University, he became a curate in Essex, Shropshire and then Yorkshire. Patrick Brontë and Maria Branwell married in 1812 in Yorkshire, and in the next eight years Maria gave birth to five daughters and one son.

- Charlotte, Emily and Anne were born in 1816, 1818 and 1820 respectively. They had two older sisters, Maria and Elizabeth, and a brother, Branwell, born in 1817.

- In 1820, the family moved from the village of Thornton to the parsonage at Haworth on the edge of the moors because Patrick Brontë became curate of the parish. Tabitha Ackroyd (called 'Taby' in Emily's diary) worked as the family servant.

- Maria Branwell Brontë, Emily's mother, died of cancer in 1821. Elizabeth Branwell, Mrs Brontë's sister (known to the Brontë children as Aunt Branwell) came from Cornwall to live with the family and look after them.

- In 1824 Maria, Elizabeth, Charlotte and Emily were sent to school at Cowan Bridge, thirty miles from Haworth. In 1825 Maria and Elizabeth died from an outbreak of typhus fever at the school. Emily and Charlotte returned home in 1825 and were taught by their aunt.

- In 1831 Charlotte was sent away to Roe Head School. She remained there until May 1832. In May 1835 she returned to the school as a teacher, accompanied by Emily and later Anne, who were pupils. Emily and Anne were both unhappy at the school and they soon returned to Haworth.

- Branwell tried, unsuccessfully, to make his living as a portrait painter. Charlotte gave up her teaching job at Roe Head in 1838 and Emily took a turn at working as a teacher in Law Hill School near Halifax. From 1839 to 1841 Anne and Charlotte took various jobs as governesses, and Branwell was employed as a tutor and as a railway clerk.

Haworth Parsonage, c. 1860

- Charlotte, Emily and Anne planned to set up their own school, but these plans were later abandoned. In 1842 Emily and Charlotte went to Brussels to improve their command of languages. They were students in the Pensionnat Héger; Monsieur Héger became a particularly influential figure for Charlotte.

- Elizabeth Branwell died in 1842. Emily and Charlotte returned to England. Later, Charlotte returned alone to Belgium and stayed until 1844.

- Branwell was often depressed; he drank heavily and smoked opium. He was dismissed from various jobs for incompetence. In 1845 he and Anne both left their teaching jobs with the Robinson family after Mr Robinson's discovery of the love affair between Branwell and Mrs Robinson.

- In 1846 the three sisters paid Aylott and Jones, a publishing company, to publish their poems. They used pseudonyms and the volume was called *Poems* by Acton, Currer and Ellis Bell. It sold only two copies.

- Later in 1846 the sisters sent their three novels (*Agnes Grey* by Anne Brontë, *The Professor* by Charlotte Brontë and *Wuthering Heights* by Emily Brontë) to a range of publishers. All three novels were, at first, rejected by the publishers.

- Charlotte Brontë's novel *Jane Eyre* was accepted for publication in 1847 and appeared in October of that year. *Wuthering Heights* and *Agnes Grey* had also been accepted by Thomas Newby and Sons, although the Brontës had to agree to pay a £50 advance to the publisher. Both novels appeared in December 1847. Anne Brontë also wrote *The Tenant of Wildfell Hall,* which was published in 1848.

Emily Brontë, a portrait by Branwell Brontë

- In January 1848 the whole Brontë family caught a serious form of influenza that killed three of them within a year. Branwell died in September 1848. Emily attended her brother's funeral, but that was the last day she left the house. Emily Brontë died of inflammation of the lungs, a symptom of tuberculosis (known in Victorian times as 'consumption'). Anne Brontë died in May 1849.

- Charlotte Brontë's novel *Shirley* was published in 1849, and in 1850 Charlotte prepared new editions of her sisters' novels *Wuthering Heights* and *Agnes Grey*. She drew upon her experiences in Belgium in the writing of her next novel, *Villette,* which was published in 1853.

- In April 1854 Charlotte Brontë became engaged to her father's curate, Arthur Nicholls. They married in the July and Charlotte's literary career ended, in part, perhaps, because her husband seems to have censored her writing. Charlotte Brontë died in March 1855. *The Professor* was published after her death.

The Brontë sisters, a portrait by Branwell Brontë (note that the figure of Branwell has been painted over)

Fragments

From the register of the Clergy Daughters' School at Cowan Bridge:

> Emily Brontë $5^3/_4$ 1824 Novbr H Cough Reads very prettily & Works a
> little Left School June 1st 1825 Governess
>> (in Chitham, 1987)

Ellen Nussey, Charlotte Brontë's friend, first visited Haworth in 1833. She described
Emily as

> an attractive girl with beautiful hair and very beautiful eyes – kind,
> kindling, liquid eyes, but she did not often look at you; she was very
> reserved ... she talked very little.
>> (in Wise and Symington, 1933, Vol. I, page 112)

Fragment of a diary written by Emily and Anne Brontë in 1834, when Emily was
sixteen years old:

> This morning Branwell went down to Mrs Driver's and brought news
> that Sir Robert Peel was going to be invited to stand for Leeds. Anne
> and I have been peeling apples for Charlotte to make an apple pudding
> ... Taby said just now Come Anne pilloputate ... Papa opened the door
> and gave Branwell a letter saying Here Branwell read this and show it to
> your Aunt and Charlotte. The Gondals are discovering the interior of
> Gaaldine. Sally Mosley is washing in the back kitchin. It is past twelve
> o'clock Anne and I have not tided ourselves, done our bedwork or done
> our lessons and we want to go out to play We are going to have for
> dinner Boiled Beef, Turnips, potatoes and apple pudding. The kitchin
> is in a very untidy state Anne and I have not done our music exercise
> which consists of *b major* Taby said on my putting a pen in her face Ya
> pitter pottering there instead of pilling a potate. I said Dear, O Dear, O
> Dear I will derectly With that I get up, take a knife and begin pilling.
> Finished pilling the potatoes Papa going to walk Mr Sutherland expected.
> Anne and I wonder what we shall be and where we shall be, if all goes
> well in the year 1874.
>> (in Wise and Symington, 1933, Vol. I, pages 124–5)

Extract from a letter written by Charlotte Brontë to her friend, Ellen Nussey, in
1837:

> My sister Emily is gone into a situation as a teacher in a large school of
> near forty pupils, near Halifax. I have had one letter from her since her
> departure; it gives an appalling account of her duties – hard labour from
> six in the morning until near eleven at night, with only one half-hour of
> exercise between. This is slavery. I fear she will never stand it.
>> (in Wise and Symington, 1933, Vol. I, page 162)

Extract from the second 'Birthday Paper' written by Emily Brontë in 1845:

> Now I don't desire a school at all, and none of us have any great longing
> for it. We have cash enough for our present wants, with a prospect of
> accumulation ... I am quite contented for myself: not as idle as formerly
> ... and having learned to make the most of the present ... seldom or
> never troubled with nothing to do, and merely desiring that everybody
> could be as comfortable as myself and as undesponding ... I must hurry
> off now to my turning and ironing.
>> (in Wise and Symington, 1933, Vol. II, page 51)

Gondal

In 1826 the Reverend Brontë bought Branwell some toy soldiers and the children began to invent stories about them. One of their main characters was the Duke of Wellington, who had defeated Napoleon at the battle of Waterloo in 1815 and became Prime Minister in 1828. Charlotte and Branwell worked together on stories and poems about the imaginary kingdom of Angria; Emily and Anne invented the kingdom of Gondal set in the North Pacific. The stories were highly dramatic adventures, full of daring deeds and romance, written in tiny handwriting on scraps of paper and in tiny books. The following is an extract from a set of verses written in 1837. Augusta, the heroine, has been freed from months of imprisonment which has almost driven her to madness:

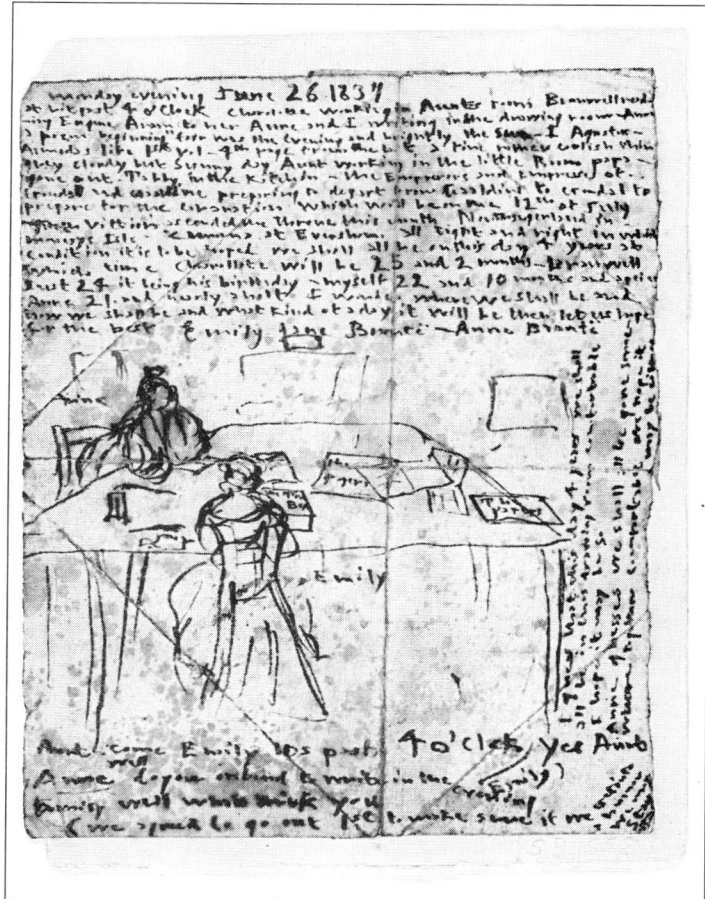

An extract from Emily Brontë's journal, 1837

O God of heaven! the dream of horror,
The frightful dream is over now;
The sickened heart, the blasting sorrow,
The ghastly night, the ghastlier morrow,
The aching sense of utter woe;

The burning tears that would keep welling
The groans that mocked at every tear
That burst from out their dreary dwelling
As if each gasp were life expelling,
But life was nourished by despair;

The tossing and the anguished pining;
The grinding teeth and staring eye;
The agony of still repining
When not a spark of hope was shining
From gloomy fate's relentless sky;

The impatient rage, the useless shrinking
From thoughts that could not be borne;
The soul that was for ever thinking,
Till nature, maddened, tortured, sinking,
At last refused to mourn –

It's over now – and I am free,
And the ocean wind is caressing me,
The wild wind that from wavy main
I never thought to see again.

First reading

Reading log

This is to provide you with a quick reference for the main events, the chronology and the narrators of *Wuthering Heights*. The first and third columns are completed for you. Use them to help you record the main facts under each of the other headings.

Decide whether Lockwood or Nelly is the narrator and put L or N in the second column. Note any information on the season, date or time of day alongside the summary of the events you are recording.

The summary for Chapter 1 has been completed to start you off.

VOLUME 1

Chapter	Narrator	Year	Season, date, time	Main events
1	L	1801	Winter, November?	Lockwood becomes the tenant at Thrushcross Grange. He visits Wuthering Heights and receives a cool reception from Heathcliff and Joseph.
2		1801		
3		1801		
4		1801/1771		
5		1776		
6		1776/1777		

Chapter	Narrator	Year	Season, date, time	Main events
7		1777		
8		1778		
9		1780		
10		1801/1783		
11		1783		
12		1784		
13		1784		
14		1784		

VOLUME 2

Chapter	Narrator	Year	Season, date, time	Main events
1 (15)*		1784		
2 (16)		1784		
3 (17)		1784		
4 (18)		1797		
5 (19)		1797		
6 (20)		1797		
7 (21)		1797–1800		
8 (22)		1800		
9 (23)		1800		

*Some modern editions of *Wuthering Heights* retain the original two-volume format. Other editions number the chapters from 1 to 34.

Chapter	Narrator	Year	Season, date, time	Main events
10 (24)		1800		
11 (25)		1801/1800		
12 (26)		1800		
13 (27)		1800		
14 (28)		1800		
15 (29)		1800		
16 (30)		1801		
17 (32)		1802		
18 (33)		1802		
19 (34)		1802		

Telling comments

As you read *Wuthering Heights* for the first time, keep a note of quotations which seem to you to reveal something about each of the two narrators, Nelly and Lockwood.

- Keep one page for Nelly and one for Lockwood.

- Divide each page into two main columns. In the first column, jot down any quotations which are revealing about the narrator's attitudes, values, personality or previous history. Make sure you include the page reference, and try to select a short passage (even a few words) which makes the point.

- In the second column, make a note of what characteristics or points you think are revealed.

For example:

Lockwood

'A perfect misanthropist's Heaven – and Mr Heathcliff and I are such a suitable pair to divide the desolation between us.' (page 3)	*L. thinks he wants to get away from people, but he immediately starts looking around for company.*
'I felt interested in a man who seemed more exaggeratedly reserved than myself.' (page 3)	*L. doesn't seem shy, though he thinks he is. H. doesn't seem shy – he seems rude. Perhaps L. isn't a very good judge of character?*
'She was not a gossip, I feared, unless about her own affairs, and those could hardly interest me.' (page 33)	*L. is inquisitive, and a snob.*

Nelly

'I was almost always at Wuthering Heights; because my mother had nursed Mr Hindley Earnshaw ...' (page 35)	*N. has had a connection with the Earnshaw family all her life.*
'They entirely refused to have it [i.e. Heathcliff] in bed with them, or even in their room, and I had no more sense, so, I put it on the landing of the stairs, hoping it might be gone on the morrow.' (page 37)	*N. as a young woman unsympathetic and narrow minded towards a young child. Calls him 'it'. Seems to feel superstitious about him? That he could be 'magicked away'?*

- As you work through the book, stop regularly to review your impressions of each narrator. Compare your quotations and comments with other people's in your group. Add to your own notes if you are convinced by other people's points.

When you have finished reading

This is to help you pull together your judgements and ideas about Nelly and Lockwood and record them in a way you can refer to easily.

- Divide into groups: one to consider Nelly and one to consider Lockwood.

- Pool your ideas about the character you are working on. List the characteristics and qualities the character shows throughout the novel.

- Group the ideas into related sets, within circles. Add the page references for the judgements as 'legs' on the spider diagrams (see below for examples).

  Remember, a character might show contradictory characteristics at different times.

- Share your work with the other group. Keep copies for reference and revision.

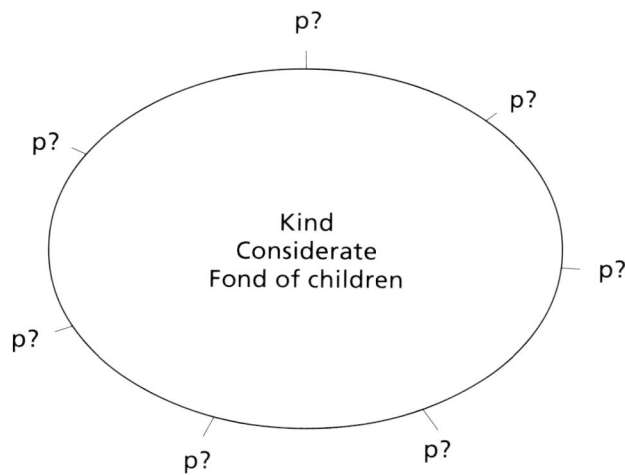

NELLY

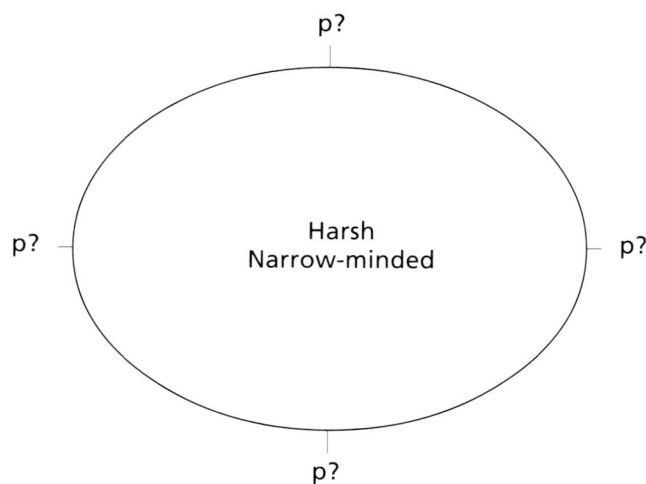

After reading

Characters

Family tree

On the opposite page you will find a skeleton diagram of the family tree for the two interrelated families in *Wuthering Heights* to which the main characters belong: the Earnshaws and the Lintons. The names of characters and dates of marriages have been left out.

- Using the character names below, complete the family tree.

- Add marriage dates from the list on this page.

- Add further information to complete the family tree, e.g. each character's family name(s), ages at marriages and at deaths.

- Look carefully at the structure of the family tree. What patterns do you notice? How important do you think this patterning is in *Wuthering Heights*?

Characters

Mr Earnshaw *d.* Oct 1777	Heathcliff *b.* 1764 *d.* May 1802
Isabella *b.* late 1765 *d.* July 1797	Edgar *b.* 1762 *d.* Sept 1801
Mr Linton *d.* Autumn 1780	Mrs Earnshaw *d.* Spring or Summer 1773
Catherine *b.* Summer 1765 *d.* 20 Mar 1784	Hareton *b.* June 1778
Hindley *b.* 1757 *d.* Sept 1784	Catherine *b.* 20 Mar 1784
Linton *b.* Sept 1784 *d.* Sept 1801	Mrs Linton *d.* Autumn 1780 Frances *d.* late 1778

Marriage dates

March 1783
January 1784
September 1801
1 January 1803

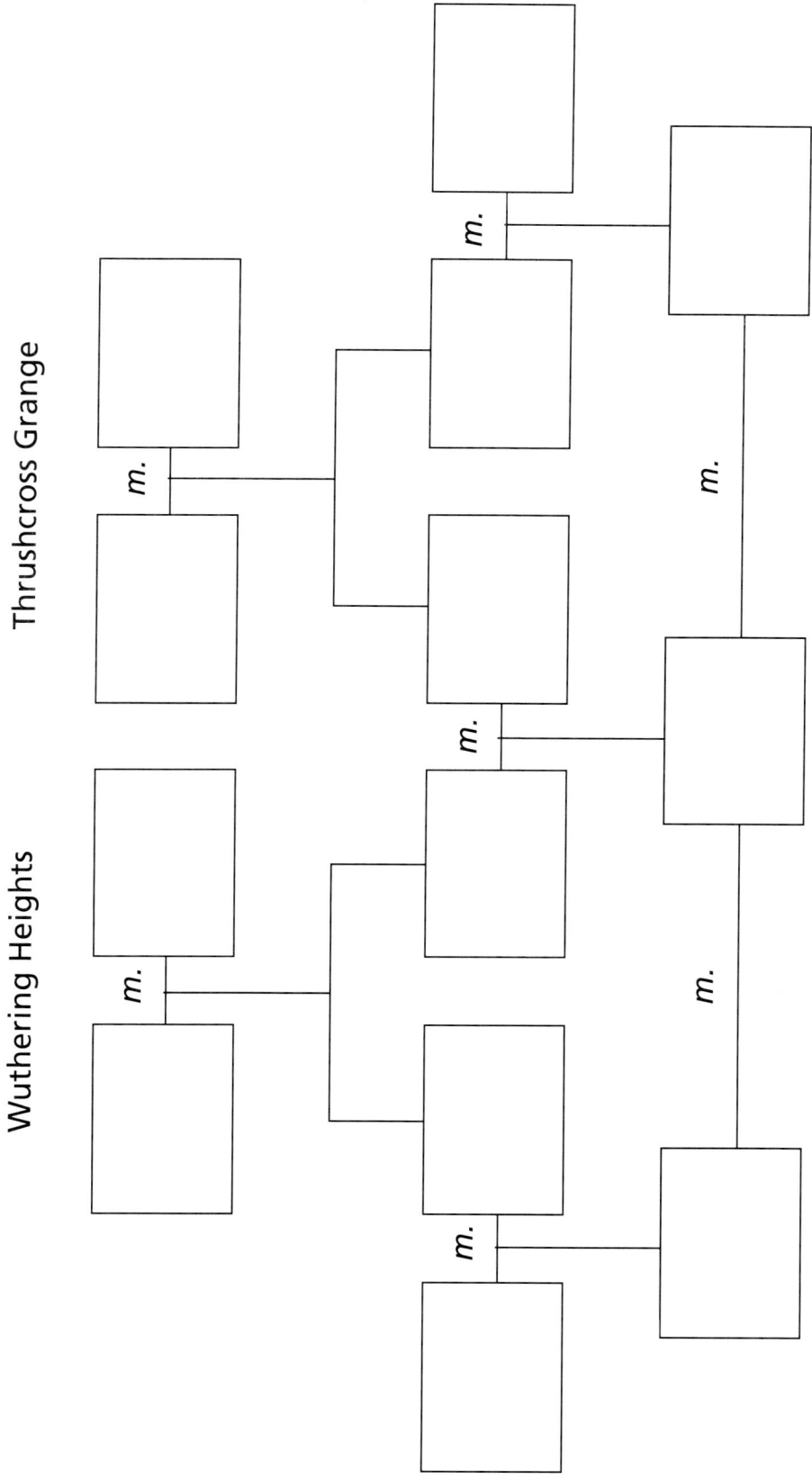

Thrushcross Grange

Wuthering Heights

m.

m.

m.

m.

m.

m.

m.

Character constructs

The point of this exercise, which is based on a procedure used in psychological testing, is to help you draw out interesting ideas about the way you see the characters in *Wuthering Heights*. These ideas, or 'constructs', should help you consider the links between characters and their roles within the thematic structure of the novel.

1. Write each character's name on a separate slip of paper.

2. Pick out any three names and try to think of a way in which two of the characters are similar and the third character is different. For example, if you picked out Isabella, Joseph and Nelly Dean, you might note that Joseph and Nelly are servants, whereas Isabella is from a wealthy, land-owning family. Or you might observe that Nelly and Isabella have each lived at both Thrushcross Grange and Wuthering Heights, and both have effectively been kept prisoner at Wuthering Heights at some point. Joseph, by contrast, lives only at Wuthering Heights, willingly, until his threat to leave at the end of the novel.

3. Note down the ideas you come up with, like this:

Nelly
Joseph } servants ——————————————— wealthy } Isabella

Nelly
Isabella } live in both houses ——————— lives only at Wuthering Heights } Joseph

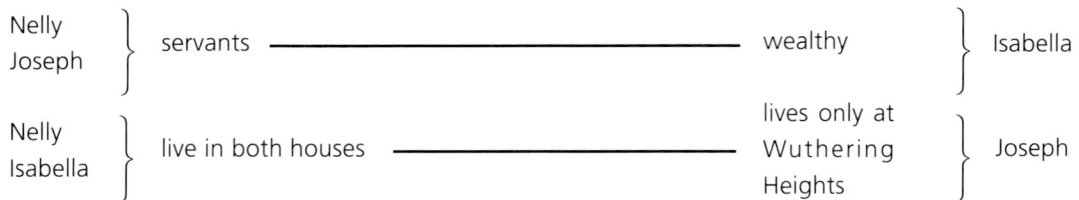

4. Return the slips of paper to the pile and repeat the exercise for another three characters. Continue in this way until you have elicited 10–15 ideas which you think are interesting, revealing or important about the novel. (The illustrations given above, for example, would give you the chance to consider the importance of social class as an idea affecting different characters, the extent to which different characters are associated with different places the novel, and the theme of imprisonment.)

5. Compare your findings with a partner's. Make sure that you have noted down the ideas that have arisen.

Catherine and Heathcliff

The passages listed below have been chosen because they show Catherine and Heathcliff at turning points in their lives. Through close textual analysis of each passage, focus on how each character is presented at these key moments. Consider:

- what immediately precedes the extract

- what happens after it

- whose point of view it is written from

- what evidence it offers about character and motivation

- any notable points about the language or imagery used.

1. Annotate each extract as fully as possible with your own comments and questions.

2. Compare notes with other group members. Add to your own written comments.

We have started annotating one extract as an example.

Immediately before this, Cathy and Heathcliff have been discovered spying on the Lintons at the Grange. Cathy has been bitten by Skulker

Potential violence symbolised here. Heathcliff has the power to shatter and fragment the domestic picture

Cathy has a spiteful and vindictive streak

Heathcliff voices his total admiration for Cathy

Anecdote is narrated by Heathcliff but Nelly is remembering his words to narrate them to Lockwood. Heathcliff is an outsider looking in. Symbolically important – he will remain on the outside of this household

Emphasises social class difference between Heathcliff and the Lintons

Cathy enjoys the attention

The Lintons seem foolish, empty people to Heathcliff, without spirit

Heathcliff naïve and open at this stage

'The curtains were still looped up at one corner; and I resumed my station as spy, because, if Catherine had wished to return, I intended shattering their great glass panes to a million of fragments, unless they let her out.

'She sat on the sofa quietly: Mrs Linton took off the grey cloak of the dairy maid which we had borrowed for our excursion, shaking her head, and expostulating with her, I suppose; she was a young lady and they made a distinction between her treatment and mine. Then the woman servant brought a basin of warm water, and washed her feet; and Mr Linton mixed a tumbler of negus, and Isabella emptied a plate of cakes into her lap, and Edgar stood gaping at a distance. Afterwards, they dried and combed her beautiful hair, and gave her a pair of enormous slippers, and wheeled her to the fire, and I left her, as merry as she could be, dividing her food between the little dog and Skulker, whose nose she pinched as she ate; and kindling a spark of spirit in the vacant blue eyes of the Lintons – a dim reflection from her own enchanting face – I saw they were full of stupid admiration; she is so immeasurably superior to them – to everybody on earth; is she not, Nelly?'

Passages for analysis

We crowded round, and, over Miss Cathy's head ... because he was determined he would not leave it as he found it. (pages 36–7)

Miss Cathy and he were now very thick ... though hardness, not gentleness, made him give little trouble. (page 38)

She, supposing Edgar could not see her, snatched the cloth from my hand ... and enabled them to forsake the disguise of friendship, and confess themselves lovers. (pages 70–72)

'I tell you I won't harken to your dreams, Miss Catherine! ... and Linton's is as different as a moonbeam from lightning, or frost from fire.' (page 80)

Now fully revealed by the fire and candlelight, I was amazed ... and you must forgive me, for I struggled only for you!' (pages 95–6)

'By no means!' cried Mrs Linton in answer ...'She's her brother's heir, is she not?' he asked, after a brief silence. (pages 104–5)

'To get rid of me – answer my question,' persevered Mr Linton ... 'She has blood on her lips!' he said, shuddering. (pages 116–7)

Heathcliff had knelt on one knee to embrace her ... that will be worse to remember than my harsh words! (pages 158–9)

'May she wake in torment!' he cried ... It hardly moved my compassion – it appalled me; still I felt reluctant to quit him so. (page 167)

Hareton and Catherine

This task builds upon the work you have been doing on Catherine and Heathcliff. The focus is upon Hareton and the younger Catherine.

1. First, look through the parts of the book in which Hareton and Catherine feature. Select two short passages which seem to you to be particularly significant in highlighting turning points in the characters' development.

2. Prepare some notes to remind you of your main points about each passage. The guidelines for the textual analysis on Catherine and Heathcliff might help you here. Consider:

   ■ what immediately precedes the extract you have chosen

   ■ what happens after it

   ■ whose point of view it is written from

   ■ what evidence it offers about character and motivation

   ■ any notable points about the language or imagery used.

3. Work with a partner who has selected different passages. Set each other the two passages to read and annotate.

4. Read and comment upon your partner's work. Discuss the similarities and differences in your points of view. Were the passages well chosen? What have you learned about the characters and their roles in the novel?

Minor characters

This section of work is to help you consider the following questions:

- How well drawn are the minor characters in *Wuthering Heights?* What does each character contribute to the novel?

Here is a list of the minor characters. Divide the list between your group so that you research the whole list between you.

- Joseph
- Zillah
- Doctor Kenneth
- Frances.

Consider the following questions. Make notes and keep page references.

- What biographical information is the reader given about the character? (Where does s/he live? What do we know about his or her life?)

- How does the character speak? Does Emily Brontë use mainly direct or reported speech to convey the character? What does the character's use of language contribute to the atmosphere or tone or pace of the novel?

- Is the character significant in moving the plot forward at any point? If so, when and why?

- Does the character provide an opportunity for a more major character to be shown in a new light?

- Does the character seem to you to contribute to any particular theme in the novel?

Pull your ideas together by preparing a handout and giving a short talk on your character to the rest of the group.

Places

Map

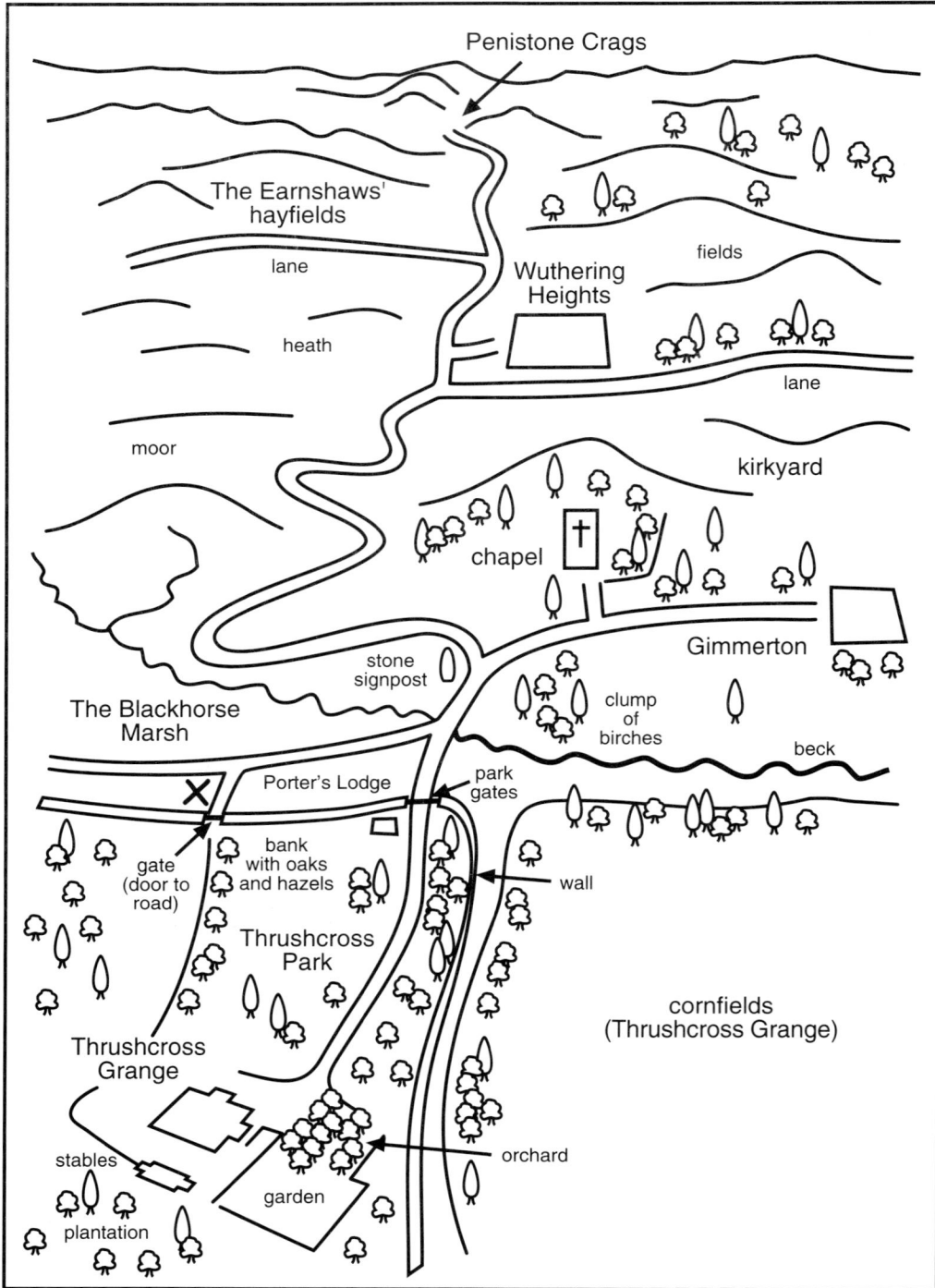

> I came to a stone where the highway branches off on to the moor at your left hand; a rough sand-pillar, with the letters W.H. cut on its north side, on the east, G., and on the south-west, T.G. It serves as guide-post to the Grange, and Heights, and village.
>
> (page 107)

There is enough information in the novel about the relative locations of Wuthering Heights, Thrushcross Grange and other places to be able to draw a sketch map of the local area. On a copy of the map opposite, or on a map you have sketched yourself, use a key to show main events associated with each location. You will find it helpful to refer to your reading log.

As an example, (x) on the map by the door in the wall of Thrushcross Park shows where Cathy loses her hat over the wall and encounters Heathcliff (page 229).

Obviously there will be too many events to show at Wuthering Heights and Thrushcross Grange, so decide on a few important ones.

Wuthering Heights and Thrushcross Grange

Given the significance of the two houses in Wuthering Heights, and the use of the name of one of them as the title, it is valuable to explore exactly how both Wuthering Heights and Thrushcross Grange are presented and used in the novel.

You will find it useful to work in pairs for this activity.

1. Compare the two quotations below. Which house is described in each, and at what point in the story?

   > There was a carpet, a good one; but the pattern was obliterated by dust; a fire-place hung with cut paper dropping to pieces; a handsome oak-bedstead with ample crimson curtains of rather expensive material, and modern make. But they had evidently experienced rough usage: the valance hung in festoons, wrenched from their rings, and the iron rod supporting them was bent in an arc, on one side, causing the drapery to trail upon the floor. The chairs were also damaged, many of them severely; and deep indentations deformed the panels of the walls.

   > … a splendid place carpeted with crimson, and crimson-covered chairs and tables, and a pure white ceiling bordered by gold, a shower of glass-drops hanging in silver chains from the centre, and shimmering with little soft tapers.

2. Find further quotations that describe each house: its interior, exterior and surroundings.

3. In your pair, each take one house and write a commentary, using your quotations and the reading log completed earlier. Use the following questions as a guide.

   - How is the house and setting described, in terms of physical details and imagery?

   - What is the house's history: which characters are associated with it at different times, and what is their relationship to it (e.g. owner, tenant, servant)?

   - How does the house change, and why?

   - What is the symbolic significance of the house in the novel?

4. Respond to one another's work, adding further details and comments.

5. Working together, draft a short piece of writing (between 50 and 100 words) summarising what you have found out about the importance of the two houses and the contrasts between them.

When you have completed this work, you might like to discuss the following question, which could be set in an examination or for coursework:

- What is the significance of the title of *Wuthering Heights?*

Use the map to help you identify other significant places in the novel. You could then use a similar approach to the one you have just used to look at the two houses to consider the ways in which other places are presented in the novel. An example might be the church:

> The grey church looked greyer, and the lonely churchyard lonelier. I distinguished a moor sheep cropping the short turf on the graves.

Themes

1. Begin this work by thinking about **oppositions** and **dichotomies** in *Wuthering Heights*. Work in a pair or small group to brainstorm your ideas.

   - Start with the characters. Do any of them seem paired as opposites?

   - Now think about places – for example, Thrushcross Grange and Wuthering Heights. Are there others?

   - Now try to think in a more abstract way; are there any ideas or emotions that seem oppositional?

     > Examples might be *life* and *death*; *nature* and *culture*; *imprisonment* and *escape*; *marriage* and *passion*.

2. As a whole group, make one list of the oppositions you can detect in the text. (Some ideas and suggestions will overlap – decide on the wording that best represents your discussions.)

3. In your pairs or small groups, pick the most interesting and significant oppositions and try to break them down further, into more easily defined ideas.

   > For example, *nature* and *culture* might be seen as oppositional within the text. Thinking more about it, you might decide that this opposition included the following ideas:
   >
   > - *being wild* versus *being tame*
   >
   > - *domesticity* versus *living without comforts and social trappings*
   >
   > - *being polite* versus *following your instincts*
   >
   > - *being educated* versus *being uneducated*
   >
   > - *being at one with the natural surroundings* versus *being protected from the natural surroundings.*

Clearly, there are no right and wrong answers here – it's a matter of your own interpretation of the novel. Nevertheless, you have to be able to support your way of seeing the opposition by referring to the text.

4. Look back at the list of oppositions you have generated. The task now is to try to decide whether, in *Wuthering Heights*, one side of the opposition is portrayed as being more positive than the other.

> This might be a difficult decision to arrive at, but try to make a general judgment. For example, if we took
>
> ■ *being educated* versus *being uneducated*
>
> the positive side of the opposition would probably be being educated. Hareton's life is being improved by education at the end of the novel; Heathcliff goes away and returns with an education which gives him increased power … There are plenty of examples to support this.
>
> *Being polite* versus *following your instincts* is perhaps harder to decide upon. Generally, though, our view is that the author suggests that following instincts is more important and positive than keeping to good manners. We would justify this in relation to Catherine and Heathcliff's relationship, and especially the deathbed scene.
>
> So, our positive/negative list of oppositions for the example we gave in question 3 looks like this:
>
> | **Positive** | **Negative** |
> |---|---|
> | being educated | being uneducated |
> | following your instincts | being polite |
> | being wild | being tame |
> | domesticity | living without comforts and social trappings |
> | being at one with the natural surroundings | being protected from the natural surroundings |

Work through the oppositions you have noted, drawing up a table of positives and negatives like the one shown here.

5. Now look again at the 'positive' column.

■ First, group the ideas that seem to you to link together comfortably. In our example, we would link *being wild*, *following your instincts*, and *being at one with the natural surroundings*. *Domesticity* and *being educated* would be grouped separately.

■ Then, decide whether you think there are any tensions between the different groups of 'positive' ideas. If so, what are these tensions? How do they relate to the novel as a whole?

In our example, there is an obvious tension between the two groups of ideas. This tension is particularly obvious in Catherine's life, in the choices she makes – to marry, to live at Thrushcross Grange whilst retaining her commitment to the wildness and instinctiveness of her relationship with Heathcliff. The same tension can be seen in Hareton's life, and in Heathcliff's (represented in the story by the absence during which he acquires an education). The tension was also one which related to Emily Brontë's own life and circumstances.

- Repeat this exercise with your 'negative' column.

- Which oppositions were most difficult to place in the positive or negative column? Can you suggest why?

6. Identifying and writing about themes

You need now to produce a structured piece of writing about each of the major themes of the novel. Arrange, if you can, to collaborate with other members of your group to produce this work, but remember that you need to have thought through and understood how each of these major ideas works in *Wuthering Heights*.

Begin by looking back at your answer to question 2, in which you listed the major oppositions you see in the novel. This list will give you the basis of deciding which themes you think are most important in the novel. Your answers to questions 3, 4 and 5 will help you examine and discuss these themes.

Use the checklist below on your own (or other people's) writing to make sure that the main points have been covered:

- identify the theme you are discussing

- show how the theme is developed:
  - which characters are most important to it?
  - which locations?
  - which elements of the plot?
  - does the structure of the novel develop it (e.g. by repeating an idea, or reworking it differently)?

- discuss the value that seems to be attached to different ideas within the theme. Does the way the novel has been written lead you to favour a particular set of ideas?

- show how the theme links with other themes and ideas that are important to the novel.

Motifs

There are three stages to this method of examining motifs in *Wuthering Heights*. We have illustrated the process by considering one of the most striking motifs in the text – windows.

Choose one or more of the following to work at in a similar manner: **eyes**, **dreams**, **thresholds**, **daylight**, **books**, **animals**. Add to this list as you think of other recurring images.

1. Building a diagram

Firstly, produce a diagram similar to the one below. On the inner circle consider any events or references which relate to the motif. When you have done this, move to the outer circle and write down any key ideas that relate to the references in the inner circle.

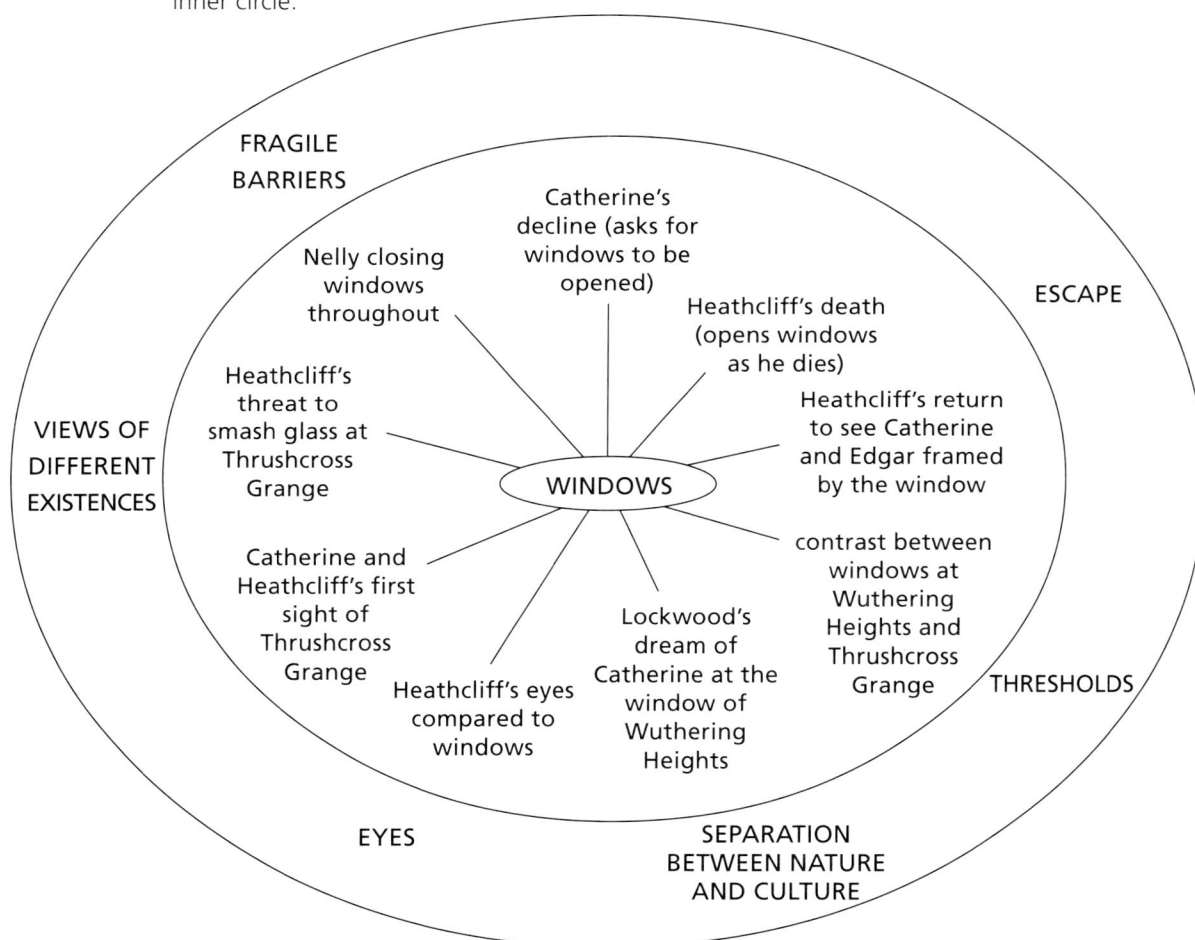

FRAGILE BARRIERS

Nelly closing windows throughout

Catherine's decline (asks for windows to be opened)

Heathcliff's death (opens windows as he dies)

ESCAPE

VIEWS OF DIFFERENT EXISTENCES

Heathcliff's threat to smash glass at Thrushcross Grange

Heathcliff's return to see Catherine and Edgar framed by the window

WINDOWS

Catherine and Heathcliff's first sight of Thrushcross Grange

contrast between windows at Wuthering Heights and Thrushcross Grange

Heathcliff's eyes compared to windows

Lockwood's dream of Catherine at the window of Wuthering Heights

THRESHOLDS

EYES

SEPARATION BETWEEN NATURE AND CULTURE

2. Drafting

Swap diagrams with someone who has chosen a different motif. Use your partner's diagrams to write up a page on a new motif. Start by producing a first draft of some writing on the motif, using the diagram to help you describe the main references and their connotations. For example:

Windows are an important motif in Wuthering Heights. They provide a separation between what is outdoors and indoors, between nature and

culture. They allow views of alternative lives, as when Catherine and Heathcliff first visit Thrushcross Grange and watch the Lintons through the window. The moors towards Wuthering Heights can be seen from the large windows of Thrushcross Grange.

The opening and closing of windows is significant, as when Catherine asks Nelly to close the window after Heathcliff leaves. She and Edgar are sitting in a window when Heathcliff later returns. When Lockwood spends a night at Wuthering Heights the window has been soldered shut and he breaks the glass when Catherine appears to him at the window in his dream. Both Catherine and Heathcliff want windows open as they approach death and when Heathcliff dies his window is open on to the moor.

Eyes, particularly Heathcliff's, are described as windows ...

3. Revising

Produce a second draft of your writing building in detailed references to the novel. Revise the language and shape the work into a suitable form for a short essay. Obviously, this example is not complete, and the motif of windows is not exhaustively explored, but this shows how the piece of writing might be developed.

Windows are an important motif in Wuthering Heights. Like other forms of threshold, they provide a separation between what is outdoors and indoors, between nature and culture, but they are a transparent and fragile barrier. They allow views of alternative existences, as when Catherine and Heathcliff first visit Thrushcross Grange and watch the Lintons through the window: 'they had not put up the shutters and the curtains were only half closed. Both of us were able to look in by standing on the basement and clinging on the ledge, and we saw – ah! it was beautiful – a splendid place ... we should have thought ourselves in heaven!' Later, anxious that Catherine might be held by the Lintons against her will, Heathcliff 'intended shattering their great glass panes to a million of fragments, unless they let her out.' The moors towards Wuthering Heights can be seen from the windows of Thrushcross Grange, but the farm itself, whose 'narrow windows are deeply set' is not visible.

The opening and closing of windows is significant, as when Catherine asks Nelly to close the window the morning after Heathcliff leaves Wuthering Heights. When he returns to Thrushcross Grange three years later he looks up to the windows 'which reflected a score of glittering moons, but showed no light from within.' Inside, Catherine and Edgar are sitting at the window looking out over the valley of Gimmerton, but the curtains are closed on this 'wonderously peaceful' scene as Heathcliff enters.

Windows also represent the separation between life and death, broken by violence and desperate passion. When Lockwood spends a night at Wuthering Heights the window hook had been 'soldered into the staple,' but he breaks the glass when the child's face appears to him at the window in his dream, and 'pulled its wrist on to the broken pane, and rubbed it to and fro'. On hearing of Lockwood's dream, Heathcliff 'wrenched open the lattice, bursting ... into an uncontrollable passion of tears.'...

Narrative structure

How the story is told

Using the reading log you created earlier, you should now examine in more detail exactly how the story of *Wuthering Heights* is told. In order to understand the narrative structure more fully, consider your response to these two important questions:

- Who tells the story of *Wuthering Heights?*

- How is time used?

Emily Brontë's principal device is the use of Lockwood and Ellen Dean as main narrators. Lockwood's is the framing narrative, telling of his two visits to Thrushcross Grange in 1801 and 1802, and he provides an audience for Ellen Dean. She relates most of the events, from Heathcliff's arrival in 1771 to his death in 1802, directly to Lockwood. This narrative structure uses the intersecting chronologies of 1801–2 and 1771–1802 in a flashback-like way. However, events are not always told strictly chronologically, nor are Lockwood's and Nelly's the only viewpoints.

For each of the eight extracts on the following two pages, answer these questions:

- Whose **point of view** is this?

- Who is the notional **audience**, if there is one?

- What **form** does the episode from which this extract is taken have (e.g. diary)?

- What **part of the story** is told in this episode?

- What is the **time relationship** between this episode and the surrounding narrative?

> Joseph was bending over the fire, peering into a large pan that swung above it; and a wooden bowl of oatmeal stood on the settle close by. The contents of the pan began to boil, and he turned to plunge his hand into the bowl; I conjectured that this preparation was probably for our supper, and, being hungry, I resolved it should be eatable – so crying out sharply, '*I'll* make the porridge!' – I removed the vessel out of his reach, and proceeded to take off my hat and riding habit. 'Mr Earnshaw,' I continued, 'directs me to wait on myself – I will – I'm not going to act the lady among you, for fear I should starve.'
>
> 'Goòid Lord!' he muttered, sitting down, and stroking his ribbed stockings from the knee to the ankle.

> Once or twice, after we had gone to bed, I've happened to open my door again, and seen her sitting crying, on the stairs' top; and then I've shut myself in, quick, for fear of being moved to interfere. I did pity her then, I'm sure; still I didn't wish to lose my place, you know!
>
> At last one night she came boldy into my chamber, and frightened me out of my wits, by saying –
>
> 'Tell Mr Heathcliff that his son is dying – I'm sure he is, this time. – Get up, instantly, and tell him!'
>
> Having uttered this speech, she vanished again. I lay a quarter of an hour listening and trembling – Nothing stirred – the house was quiet.

We made ourselves as snug as our means allowed in the arch of the dresser. I had just fastened our pinafores together, and hung them up for a curtain, when in comes Joseph, on an errand from the stables. He tears down my handywork, boxes my ears, and croaks:

'T' maister nobbut just buried, and Sabbath nut o'ered, und t' sahnd uh t' gospel still i' yer lugs, and yah darr be laiking! shame on ye! sit ye dahn, ill childer! they's good books eneugh if ye'll read 'em; sit ye dahn, and think uh yer sowls!'

Saying this, he compelled us to square our positions that we might receive, from the far-off fire, a dull ray to show us the text of lumber he thrust upon us.

The day she was buried there came a fall of snow. In the evening I went to the churchyard. It blew bleak as winter – all round was solitary: I didn't fear that her fool of a husband would wander up the den so late – and no one else had business to bring them there.

Being alone and conscious two yards of loose earth was the sole barrier between us, I said to myself –

'I'll have her in my arms again! If she be cold, I'll think it is the north wind that chills me; and if she be motionless, it is sleep.'

I got a spade from the toolhouse, and began to delve with all my might – it scraped the coffin; I fell to work with my hands; the wood commenced cracking about the screws, I was on the point of attaining my object, when it seemed that I heard a sigh from some one above, close at the edge of the grave and bending down.

'Con-trary!' said a voice, as sweet as a silver bell – 'That for the third time, you dunce! I'm not going to tell you again – Recollect, or I pull your hair!'

'Contrary, then,' answered another, in deep, but softened tones. 'And now, kiss me, for minding so well.'

'No, read it over first correctly, without a single mistake.'

The male speaker began to read – he was a young man, respectably dressed, and seated at a table, having a book before him. His handsome features glowed with pleasure, and his eyes kept impatiently wandering from the page to a small white hand over his shoulder, which recalled him by a smart slap on the cheek, whenever its owner detected such signs of inattention.

'I'll not hold my tongue!' I said, 'You mustn't touch him … Let the door remain shut and be quiet!'

'No! I've formed my resolution, and by God, I'll execute it!' cried the desperate being. 'I'll do you a kindness in spite of yourself, and Hareton justice! And you needn't trouble your head to screen me, Catherine is gone – Nobody alive would regret me, or be ashamed, though I cut my throat this minute – and it's time to make and end!'

I might as well have struggled with a bear, or reasoned with a lunatic. The only resource left me was to run to a lattice, and warn his intended victim of the fate which awaited him.

'You'd better seek shelter somewhere else to-night!' I exclaimed in a rather triumphant tone.

He pulled me under the chandelier, and Mrs Linton placed her spectacles on her nose and raised her hands in horror. The cowardly children crept nearer also, Isabella lisping –

'Frightful thing! Put him in the cellar, papa. He's exactly like the son of the fortune-teller, that stole my tame pheasant. Isn't he, Edgar?'

While they examined me, Cathy came round; she heard the last speech, and laughed. Edgar Linton, after an inquisitive stare, collected sufficient wit to recognise her. They see us at church, you know, though we seldom meet them elsewhere.

'That's Miss Earnshaw!' he whispered to his mother, 'and look how Skulker has bitten her – how her foot bleeds!'

'Miss Earnshaw? Nonsense!' cried the dame, 'Miss Earnshaw scouring the country with a gypsy! And yet, my dear, the child is in mourning – surely it is – and she may be lamed for life!'

I trotted up their garden, and was turning round to the back, when that fellow Earnshaw met me, took my bridle, and bid me go in by the front entrance. He patted Minny's neck, and said she was a bonny beast, and appeared as if he wanted me to speak to him. I only told him to leave my horse alone, or it would kick him.

He answered in his vulgar accent.

'It wouldn't do mitch hurt if it did;' and surveyed its legs with a smile.

I was half inclined to make it try; however, he moved off to open the door, and said, with a stupid mixture of awkwardness and elation:

'Miss Catherine! I can read yon, nah.'

'Wonderful,' I exclaimed. 'Pray let us hear you – you are grown clever!'

Why tell the story in this way?

On the following page are twenty statements about the way in which the story of *Wuthering Heights* is told.

1. Working in pairs, copy the statements onto a sheet of paper, and cut the sheet so that each statement appears on a separate slip of paper. Sort the statements into three categories:

   Agree   **Unsure**   **Disagree**

2. For each statement, give a reason for your decision and provide evidence from the text as support.

3. Compare your categories and reasons with those of another pair. Do you notice any differences?

4. Use your ideas from this exercise to produce a piece of writing in response to the following question:

   ■ What does *Wuthering Heights* gain or lose from having more than one narrator?

You might also like to consider the following questions:

■ What is the effect of Nelly's retrospective account of events for the main part of the story?

■ How are Lockwood's direct accounts at the beginning and end of the novel different from Nelly's narrative?

■ How would the 'story' be different if it were all told as a first-person narrative by another character (e.g. Heathcliff) or in the third person, by an omniscient narrator?

■ How many narrators do you think there are in the novel? How have you decided whether a character is a narrator or not?

1. The narrative structure of *Wuthering Heights* is more complicated than it needs to be.	2. Lockwood is not absolutely essential to the novel.
3. Nelly's conversations with Lockwood are an awkward reminder of the artificiality of the novel.	4. It is important that we are able to read parts of Cathy's diary.
5. The use of retrospective narration allows a fuller understanding of events and characters.	6. The novel would be more powerful if Catherine and Heathcliff narrated more of the story.
7. There are two narrators in *Wuthering Heights*.	8. The way in which time is used is the most compelling aspect of the novel.
9. Lockwood is reliable as the main narrator because he is an impartial stranger.	10. Emily Brontë encourages us to disagree with both Nelly and Lockwood.
11. Nelly is more than a narrator, she also has a part to play in the plot of the novel.	12. Lockwood is unaffected by the story he hears.
13. The different points of view in the novel mean that we are free to make up our own minds about characters and events.	14. Nelly is the most reliable narrator.
15. Isabella's letter adds interest but is not essential to the story.	16. *Wuthering Heights* can only be understood if it is read more than once.
17. Lockwood's second visit is a clever device which adds to the impact of the story.	18. No one narrator has a full understanding of all the characters.
19. The time structure of the novel creates dramatic interest but is ultimately confusing.	20. Nelly's perspective is closely related to that of Emily Brontë herself.

Key episodes

We have chosen four key episodes from *Wuthering Heights* for you to consider in more detail. Make detailed annotations of each passage in response to each of the following points:

■ Who is narrating and whose point of view is given?

■ What is notable about the style here (e.g. diction, imagery) and what is the effect of the way the passage is written?

■ How does this passage reflect themes or motifs found in *Wuthering Heights*?

■ What is revealed about characters?

■ How important is the setting of this episode?

■ What is the context of this episode? Is the same incident referred to or echoed elsewhere in the book?

We have begun work on another passage to show you how you might do this.

Annotations (left)	Passage	Annotations (right)
Lockwood's pleasant anticipation Warm, pleasant light	Before I arrived in sight of it, all that remained of day was a beamless, amber light along the west; but I could see every pebble on the path, and every blade of grass, by that splendid moon.	Light after sunset – moon motif
	I had neither to climb the gate, nor to knock – it yielded to my hand.	Wuthering Heights easily entered – contrast to earlier visits, e.g. 'jealous gate'
Direct statement by Lockwood	That is an improvement! I thought. And I noticed another, by the aid of my nostrils; a fragrance of stocks and wall flowers wafted on the air, from amongst the homely fruit trees.	Flowers and fruit not previously associated with Wuthering Heights. Symbol of change
Window and threshold motifs – open	Both doors and lattices were open; and, yet, as is usually the case in a coal district, a fine, red fire illumined the chimney; the comfort which the eye derives from it, renders the extra heat endurable. But the house of Wuthering Heights is so large, that the inmates have plenty of space for withdrawing out of its influence; and, accordingly, what inmates there were had stationed themselves not far from one of the windows. I could both see them and hear them talk before I entered; and, looked and listened in consequence, being moved thereto by a mingled sense of curiosity, and envy that grew as I lingered.	'Inmates' sounds anonymous and archaic – institutionalised Sense of expectation
Playful conversation – childlike – who are these people, whom Lockwood can see, but has not named?	'*Con-trary!*' said a voice, as sweet as a silver bell – 'That for the third time, you dunce! I'm not going to tell you again – Recollect, or I pull your hair!'	Another example of sense imagery: pleasant, light

Passages for analysis

'Let me get off my wet clothes, and I'll tell you about it, Nelly,' he replied ... not if I might have the privilege of flinging Joseph off the highest gable, and painting the house-front with Hindley's blood!'
(pages 47–8)

'Have you found Heathcliff, you ass?' interrupted Catherine ... and standing bonnetless and shawlless to catch as much water as she could with her hair and clothes.
(pages 83–4)

About twelve o'clock, that night, was born the Catherine you saw at Wuthering Heights, a puny, seven months' child ... how much selfishness there is even in a love like Mr Linton's, when he so regretted Catherine's blessed release!
(pages 164–5)

'And what is my father like?' he asked ... Oh, damn my soul! but that's worse than I expected – and the devil knows I was not sanguine!'
(pages 204–5)

When you have annotated the passage, you might try to write a response to this question:

- What is your reaction to this extract? What is its importance in the novel as a whole?

It would be useful to consider the same issues in relation to other significant episodes you can identify in the book.

Endings

Each of the following extracts offers an ending of some sort within the novel. Consider:

■ Which elements of the plot are concluded at this point?

■ Is the ending parallelled elsewhere in the text?

■ Does the ending suggest a new beginning?

■ Is the ending satisfying on an artistic and emotional level?

■ Are there any other 'endings' within the text?

The place of Catherine's interment, to the surprise of the villagers, was neither in the chapel, under the carved monument of the Lintons, nor yet by the tombs of her own relations, outside. It was dug on a green slope, in a corner of the kirkyard, where the wall is so low that heath and bilberry plants have climbed over it from the moor; and peat mould almost buries it. Her husband lies in the same spot, now; and they have each a simple headstone above, and a plain grey block at their feet, to mark the graves.

(page 168)

The intimacy, thus commenced, grew rapidly; though it encountered temporary interruptions. Earnshaw was not to be civilized with a wish; and my young lady was no philosopher, and no paragon of patience; but both their minds tending to the same point – one loving and desiring to esteem; and the other loving and desiring to be esteemed – they contrived in the end, to reach it.

You see, Mr Lockwood, it was easy to win Mrs Heathcliff's heart; but now, I'm glad you did not try – the crown of all my wishes will be the union of those two; I shall envy no one on their wedding day – there won't be a happier woman than myself in England!

(page 312–3)

I could not think him dead – but his face and throat were washed with rain; the bed-clothes dripped, and he was perfectly still. The lattice, flapping to and fro, had grazed one hand that rested on the sill – no blood trickled from the broken skin, and when I put my fingers to it, I could doubt no more – he was dead and stark!

I hasped the window; I combed his long black hair from his forehead; I tried to close his eyes – to extinguish, if possible, that frightful, life-like gaze of exultation, before any one else beheld it. They would not shut – they seemed to sneer at my attempts, and his parted lips and sharp, white teeth sneered too!

(page 332)

I sought, and soon discovered, the three head-stones on the slope next the moor – the middle one, grey, and half buried in heath – Edgar Linton's only harmonized by the turf and moss, creeping up its foot – Heathcliff's still bare.

I lingered round them, under that benign sky; watched the moths fluttering among the heath and hare-bells; listened to the soft wind breathing through the grass; and wondered how any one could ever imagine unquiet slumbers, for the sleepers in that quiet earth.

(page 334)

Rereading and revising

Preparing for the exam

It is worthwhile spending some time looking at past exam papers to identify the types of questions that are asked about novels. In the table on the opposite page we have identified several topic areas under which common types of exam questions could be grouped. (Of course some questions could fall within more than one topic area, but we think it is helpful to start out by looking for more straightforward topics and then to consider how there could be questions that are not so simply categorised.)

This exercise can be done on your own, but you will have more ideas if you work in groups. You need to make your own table on poster-sized paper so that you have plenty of space.

1. Add to the list of topics in the first column by thinking about the aspects of *Wuthering Heights* that you have studied and by looking through your own A level syllabus and through past exam papers.

2. Elaborate each topic, noting the different approaches or focuses that might be asked for in an exam question in the second column of the table. We have made a start on this for you.

3. When you have your topics, write any past exam questions that you have found on *Wuthering Heights* in the third column alongside the appropriate topics. We have provided some examples of possible exam questions.

4. Now have a go at writing some exam questions yourself. It is a good idea to look at the questions about other books on the exam paper to give you ideas about the type of questions that could be set on *Wuthering Heights*. This will also help you to interpret the phrasing of exam questions and to recognise how the same question might be asked in different ways. (You may find that you need more space and have to continue your lists of questions on separate paper.)

When you have generated a reasonable set of exam questions you can practise producing essay plans and writing essays under realistically timed conditions. If you have not had much practice at doing this before, then it might be helpful to start by allowing yourself more time at first and then decrease this in stages until you end up writing several essays in exactly the same amount of time that you will have in the exam.

It is, of course, very useful to compare your plans and essays with those of other students.

Practising planning is just as important as practising writing. You may not have time to write timed essays in response to all the questions you have generated, but producing a quick plan for each one would be time well spent.

Topic	Focus within topic	Exam questions
Character	individual characters	*1. Discuss the importance of Joseph in Wuthering Heights.* *2. How much sympathy do you have for Catherine Earnshaw?*
	pairs: similarities, differences	
	triangles	
	groups: women/men; W.H./T.G.	
	relationships:	
Key sections	beginning of novel	
	significant events: importance in the novel	*Look at the description of Lockwood's dream when Cathy appears. What effect does this have and how important is it?*
	interesting passages: language, perspective, etc.	
Features of the text	narrative structure: narrators, use of time	*What have you found interesting about Emily Brontë's narrative technique in the novel?*
	figurative language: imagery, motifs	
	form/genre: ghost story, tragedy, melodrama	*Is Wuthering Heights more than a gothic romance?*
Assessments of the text	your personal response	
	critical opinion	

A student's examination essay

We have reproduced here a practice examination essay written by an A level student in response to the following question:

- **How significant in the novel are the contrasts between Wuthering Heights and Thrushcross Grange?**

We have annotated the student's essay to highlight both its achievements and areas in which it could have been improved. Please remember that this essay is not intended as an example of a recommended approach or style of writing; in fact it is one of the first timed essays that this student attempted. What it does provide is a realistic model of how you can work to improve the standard of your examination essays by completing practice questions and then using tutorials and response partners to improve your style.

- Before reading the essay, spend ten minutes producing your own plan in response to this title.

    Although Wuthering Heights is the more important of the two places, and Emily Brontë draws the reader's attention to this in her choice of title for the novel, Thrushcross Grange is needed to emphasise various features of Wuthering Heights by providing a comparison. Thrushcross Grange also shows that Wuthering Heights is not typical of all houses in that area.

    The student has a sensible approach from the start: establishing the particular importance of Wuthering Heights and the significance of the contrast with Thrushcross Grange in the first paragraph. The language could also be clearer, for example, the imprecise statement 'Wuthering Heights is not typical of all the houses in that area'.

- From this introduction can you tell what will be the main points of this student's argument in the rest of the essay?

- How do you think this introduction could be improved?

    Wuthering Heights is built solidly to withstand the elements in its exposed position on the moors, '"wuthering" being a significant provincial adjective, descriptive of the atmospheric tumult to which its station is exposed in stormy weather.' Whereas Thrushcross Grange, in its more sheltered position, is more for show, 'a splendid place carpeted with crimson, and crimson covered chairs and tables'. Even the windows of Wuthering Heights are different to those of Thrushcross Grange 'the narrow windows were deeply set in the wall.'

    The second paragraph contrasts the physical settings and descriptions of the two houses, although fairly briefly.

- What would you add to this paragraph?

    Different characters are connected to the two very different places. Although Heathcliff said 'I'd not exchange, for a thousand lives, my condition here for Edgar Linton's at Thrushcross Grange', Catherine finds life there appealing, when she is forced to spend time there after being attacked by the Linton's dog. But Catherine and Heathcliff are both wilder characters like Wuthering

Heights. Catherine does not feel the same at Thrushcross Grange and is quieter while she is there. When Nelly accompanies Catherine on her next stay she is surprised that 'she behaved infinitely better than I dared to expect.' It is as if she has left part of herself at Wuthering Heights and when she is very ill she says 'He's waiting till I come home,' referring to Heathcliff and Wuthering Heights. She returns to her childhood in her state of delirium. Heathcliff prefers to live at Wuthering Heights even at the time when he owns both houses. Wuthering Heights is closer to nature, just as Catherine and Heathcliff are.

Thrushcross Grange reflects the characters of Isabella and Edgar. They are both quiet and peaceful and have been protected from life (until they meet Catherine and Heathcliff) just as Thrushcross Grange is protected by the walls it is enclosed in. After Heathcliff and Isabella are married and she goes with him to Wuthering Heights she writes a letter to Nelly in which she tells her that 'my heart returned to Thrushcross Grange in twenty-four hours after I left it.' Later when, after leaving Heathcliff, she goes back to her old house briefly she says that 'the Grange is my right home.'

What is said here is good, but this seems insubstantial for the main body of the essay. There is not enough detail about the two houses, nor about the characters associated with them, particularly the youngest generation of characters.

■ How could the sections on each house be improved?

The contrasts between Wuthering Heights and Thrushcross Grange help the reader to see the contrasts between the characters. There is 'a four miles' walk,' which allows enough distance for the differences to be realistic, but also for you to feel that they are close enough to compare.

This is a good point, which could be developed by referring to the frequent journeys, mostly on foot, made betwen the two houses, but the paragraph seems rather out of place here.

Although the contrast differs slightly according to the master of each place at the particular time, Wuthering Heights always remains a far more rough place to live in. Many strange events occur there during the novel, the first being Lockwood's dream. 'As it spoke, I discerned, obscurely, a child's face looking through the window'. Heathcliff dies in Wuthering Heights in rather mysterious circumstances and Nelly admits to Lockwood 'I don't like being left by myself in this grim house ... I shall be glad when they [Catherine and Hareton] leave it, and shift to the Grange!' Catherine and Heathcliff's ghosts are seen on the moors and also by Joseph in the house. When young Catherine and Hareton leave, Wuthering Heights will be left 'for the use of such ghosts as choose to inhabit it' and so ends the story of Wuthering Heights.

This is a much more compelling paragraph, but it misses the opportunity to comment on the change Lockwood notices in Wuthering Heights after Heathcliff's death. The identification of Heathcliff with Wuthering Heights, including through imagery, could be explored more fully.

■ What key points would you want to add at this stage in the essay?

If the reader was unable to compare Wuthering Heights and Thrushcross Grange in the novel, Wuthering Heights would not be as significant a place. Emily Brontë's deliberate contrast is both effective and necessary.

This is a very swift conclusion to the essay, and rather simple, but it does reflect the student's continued control over the argument. It is worthwhile reminding yourself that you do have to be very selective in an exam under pressure of time, and that the examiners are not expecting perfection!

- You might like to read this essay through again, annotating it yourself in more detail, considering structure, expression and textual reference.

- Discuss how successful you think this essay is. You may wish to refer to the marking criteria for your own syllabus. What advice would you give this student?

- Go back to your own plan for your essay. Would you make any changes?

- You might now like to write your own essay in timed conditions, either on this title or another (see page 39). After you have done so, work with a response partner to annotate one another's essays.

Contexts and connections

Contemporary reviews of *Wuthering Heights*

The success is not equal to the abilities of the writer; chiefly because the incidents are too coarse and disagreeable to be attractive, the very best being improbable, with a moral taint about them, and the villainy not leading to results sufficient to justify the elaborate pains taken in depicting it. The execution, however, is good.
(*Spectator*, December 1847)

In spite of much power and cleverness; in spite of its truth to life in the remote nooks and corners of England *Wuthering Heights* is a disagreeable story ... The brutal master of the lonely house on 'Wuthering Heights' – a prison which might be pictured from life – has doubtless had his prototype in those uncongenial and remote districts where human beings, like the trees, grow gnarled and dwarfed and distorted by the inclement climate; but he might have been indicated with far fewer touches, in place of so entirely filling the canvas that there is hardly a scene untainted by his presence ... If the Bells, singly or collectively, are contemplating future or frequent utterances in Fiction, let us hope that they will spare us further interiors so gloomy as the one here elaborated with such dismalness ...
(*Athenaeum*, December 1847)

This is a strange book. It is not without evidences of considerable power: but, as a whole, it is wild, confused, disjointed and improbable; and the people who make up the drama, which is tragic enough in its consequences, are savages ruder than those who lived before the days of Homer ... Heathcliff may be considered as the hero of the book, if hero there be. He is an incarnation of evil qualities; implacable hate, ingratitude, cruelty, falsehood, selfishness, and revenge ...
(*Examiner*, January 1848)

The uncultured freedom of native character presents more rugged aspects than we meet with in educated society. Its manners are not only more rough, but its passions are more violent ... It is more subject to brutal instinct than to divine reason.

It is humanity in this wild state that the author of *Wuthering Heights* essays to depict. His work is strangely original. It bears a resemblance to some of those irregular German tales in which the writers, giving the reins to their fancy, represent personages as swayed and impelled to evil by supernatural influences. But they gave spiritual identity to evil impulses, while Mr Bell more naturally shows them as the natural offspring of the unregulated heart. He displays considerable power in his creations. They all have the angularity of mis-shapen growth ...

The story shows the brutalising influence of unchecked passion. His characters are a commentary on the truth that there is no tyranny in the world like that which thoughts of evil exercise in the daring and reckless breast ... The tale ... is but a fragment, yet of colossal proportion and bearing evidence of some great design. With all its power and originality, it is so rude, so unfinished and so careless, that we are perplexed to pronounce an opinion on it or to hazard a conjecture on the future of the author. As yet it belongs to the future to decide whether he will remain a rough hewer of marble or become a great and noble sculptor.

(*Britannia*, January 1848)

Wuthering Heights is a strange sort of book, baffling all regular criticism; yet it is impossible to begin and not to finish it, and quite impossible to lay it aside afterwards and say nothing about it ... In *Wuthering Heights* the reader is shocked, disgusted, almost sickened by details of cruelty, inhumanity and the most diabolical hate and vengeance, and anon come passages of powerful testimony to the supreme power of love – even over demons in the human form. The women in the book are of a strange, fiendish-angelic nature, tantalising and terrible, and the men are indescribable out of the book itself. We strongly recommend all our readers who love novelty to get this story, for we can promise them that they have never read anything like it before.

(*Douglas Jerrold's Weekly Newspaper*, January 1848)

Charlotte Brontë defends *Wuthering Heights*

The 1850 edition of *Wuthering Heights* was edited by Charlotte Brontë after her sister's death. She included two introductory pieces of writing – a 'Biographical Notice' about 'Ellis and Acton Bell' and a preface, which begins in this way:

I have just read over *Wuthering Heights*, and, for the first time, have obtained a clear glimpse of what are termed (and, perhaps, really are) its faults; have gained a definite notion of how it appears to other people – to strangers who knew nothing of the author; who are unacquainted with the locality where the scenes of the story are laid; to whom the inhabitants, the customs, the natural characteristics of the outlying hills and hamlets in the West Riding of Yorkshire are things alien and unfamiliar.

To all such *Wuthering Heights* must appear a rude and strange production. The wild moors of the north of England can for them have no interest; the language, the manners, the very dwellings and household customs of the scattered inhabitants of those districts, must be to such readers in a great measure intelligible, and – where intelligible – repulsive. Men and women who, perhaps, naturally very calm, and with feelings moderate in degree, and little marked in kind, have been trained from their cradle to observe the utmost evenness of manner and guardedness of language, will hardly know what to make of the rough, strong utterance, the harshly manifested passions, the unbridled aversions, and headlong partialities of unlettered moorland hinds and rugged moorland squires, who have grown up untaught and unchecked, except by mentors as harsh as themselves. A large class of readers, likewise, will suffer greatly from the introduction into the pages of this work of words printed with all their letters, which it has become the custom to represent by the initial and final letter only – a blank line filling the interval. I may as well say that, for this circumstance, it is out of my power to apologize; deeming it, myself, a rational plan to write words at full length. The practice of hinting by single letters those expletives with which profane and violent persons are wont to garnish their discourse, strikes me as a proceeding which, however well meant, is weak and futile. I cannot tell what good it does – what feeling it spares – what horror it conceals.

With regard to the rusticity of *Wuthering Heights*, I admit the charge, for I feel the quality. It is rustic all through. It is moorish, and wild, and knotty as the root of heath. Nor was it natural that it should be otherwise; the author herself being a native and nursling of the moors. Doubtless, had her lot been cast in a town, her writings, if she had written at all, would have possessed another character. Even had chance or taste led her to choose a similar subject, she would have treated it otherwise. Had Ellis Bell been a lady or a gentleman accustomed to what is called 'the world,' her view of a remote and unreclaimed region, as well as of the dwellers therein, would have differed greatly from that actually taken by the homebred country girl. Doubtless it would have been wider – more comprehensive: whether it would have been more original and truthful is not so certain. As far as the scenery and locality are concerned, it could scarcely have been so sympathetic: Ellis Bell did not describe as one whose eye and taste alone found pleasure in the prospect; her native hills were far more to her than a spectacle; they were what she lived in, and by, as much as the wild birds, their tenants, or as the heather, their produce. Her descriptions, then, of natural scenery, are what they should be, and all they should be.

Where delineation of human character is concerned, the case is different. I am bound to avow that she had scarcely more practical knowledge of the peasantry amongst whom she lived, than a nun has of the country people who sometimes pass her convent gates. My sister's disposition was not naturally gregarious; circumstances favoured and fostered her tendency to seclusion; except to go to church or take a walk on the hills, she rarely crossed the threshold of home. Though her feeling for the people round was benevolent, intercourse with them she never sought; nor, with very few exceptions, ever experienced. And yet she knew them: knew their ways, their language, their family histories; she could hear of them with interest, and talk of them with detail, minute, graphic, and accurate; but *with* them she rarely exchanged a word. Hence it ensued that what her mind had gathered of the real concerning them, was too exclusively confined to those tragic and terrible traits of which, in listening to the secret annals of every rude vicinage, the memory is sometimes compelled to receive the impress. Her imagination, which was a spirit more sombre than sunny, more powerful than sportive, found in such traits material whence it wrought creations like Heathcliff, like Earnshaw, like Catherine. Having formed these beings, she did not know what she had done. If the auditor of her work, when read in manuscript, shuddered under the grinding influence of natures so relentless and implacable, of spirits so lost and fallen; if it was complained that the mere hearing of certain vivid and fearful scenes banished sleep by night, and disturbed mental peace by day, Ellis Bell would wonder what was meant, and suspect the complainant of affectation. Had she but lived, her mind would of itself have grown like a strong tree, loftier, straighter, wider-spreading, and its matured fruits would have attained a mellower ripeness and sunnier bloom; but on that mind time and experience alone could work: to the influence of other intellects, it was not amenable.

A critical history

Nineteenth-century criticism of *Wuthering Heights* tended to focus on the morality of the plot, the quality of the writing and biographical information about the author. Following Charlotte Brontë's suggestion that her sister 'did not know what she had done', much of the critical writing was concerned with Emily Brontë's inspiration and what one critic called her 'instinctive art'.[1] Biographer-critics drew links between Emily Brontë's life and the novel (for example, between the behaviour of her brother Branwell and Heathcliff).[2] As you will see from reading the extracts from contemporary reviews, many critics found the morality of the novel confusing and unsettling. Many critics acknowledged the power of the plot as well as the high quality of the writing. Literary connections were made, for example with German 'Gothic' writing, or with the Romantic poetry of Byron.[3] But, as Charlotte Brontë's preface and the contemporary reviews demonstrate, there was considerable concern about the 'coarseness' of the language used in the dialogue.

Twentieth-century criticism has been very varied. There has been an ongoing interest in the themes discussed in nineteenth-century criticism. Q.D. Leavis, for example, wrote in 1969, 'I would like to clear out of the way the confusions of the plot' and made a plea for criticism of *Wuthering Heights* 'to turn its attention to the human core of the novel, to recognise its truly human centrality. How can we fail to see that the novel is based on an interest in, concern for, and knowledge of, real life?'[4]

However, a good deal of criticism has been devoted to the formal elements of the text, particularly by the '**New Critics**' of the 1940s, 50s and 60s. Earlier critics such as C.P. Sanger wrote about the structure of *Wuthering Heights* emphasising the symmetry of family relations in the text and Emily Brontë's knowledge of the laws of private property.[5] Lord David Cecil traced the pattern of storm and calm in the novel, arguing that the central conflicts were between these two cosmological forces, between like and unlike rather than between right and wrong.[6] There has been considerable discussion about the narrative devices used, for example, about whether the dual narration makes the plot seem more believable, or whether it makes the whole thing more ambiguous.[7] There has been an emphasis on patterns of imagery, recurring symbolism, metaphors and motifs. Mark Schorer, for example, traced patterns of animal imagery related to the characters and images of fire, wind and water associated with elemental emotions.[8] Frank Goodridge used the two houses, Wuthering Heights and Thrushcross Grange, to explore metaphors of exposure and enclosure.[9] Dorothy Van Ghent considered the paired motifs of the window and the two children figures to offer an interpretation about inner and outer realities and characters' efforts to break through the barriers that separate them.[10] Other critics have argued for the significance of the structures which pattern names, family and property relations, and oppositions between daylight and dream, life and death.

Psychoanalytic criticism of *Wuthering Heights* has focused on the sexual symbolism in the novel and the relation between sexuality and death.[11] Thomas Moser's 'What is the matter with Emily Jane?' makes use of Freudian theory to interpret the window and door motifs as 'female' symbols and the key and the poker as 'male' phallic symbols. Psychoanalytic and feminist criticism have also focused on the figure of the mother in the novel.[12]

Marxist criticism of the novel grounds interpretation in the social, political and economic context of the mid nineteenth century. Arnold Kettle saw Heathcliff as a representative of the working class, functioning as a moral force to show the limitations of bourgeois characters like Edgar Linton.[13] Raymond Williams interpreted the novel as registering the social and political disturbance of the years around 1847, but saw those disturbances displaced onto the personal emotional crises the novel presents.[14] Terry Eagleton pursued similar questions of the relationship between the imaginative fiction of the Brontës and the society of their time.[15]

Modern feminist readings focus on issues of motherhood and equality, on the woman as a writer and on the relationships between *Wuthering Heights* and other literary texts. Lyn Pykett, for example, sees the unusual mixture of literary genres used in the novel, the disruptions in the narrative and its careful setting in the period up to 1801 as combining to 'produce a novel which goes back and traces both changing patterns of fiction and the emergence of new forms of the family.'[16] Sandra Gilbert argues that the novel is in some senses a female re-writing of the biblical story of the fall of man and woman told by Milton in *Paradise Lost*.[17] Camille Paglia reads the novel as a dramatisation of Emily Brontë's passion for her dead sister Maria.[18]

Deconstructive readings emphasise the view that the search for a single unified meaning to the text is pointless. Deconstructionists emphasise the ambiguities and contradictions in the text. J. Hillis Miller sums this view up in this way: 'The secret truth about *Wuthering Heights* ... is that here is no secret truth.'[19]

Examples

The following extracts have been chosen to give you the flavour of some of these very varied readings of the text.

> In its movement between generations and genres *Wuthering Heights* also traces the emergence of the modern family in idealised form. It traces the process ... by which the modern nuclear family (represented by Catherine and Hareton) replaced the larger and more loosely related household (as exemplified by various stages of domestic life at the Heights), withdrawing to a private domestic space removed from the workplace. Catherine and Hareton are shown as inhabiting this newly privatised domestic realm even before their marriage and removal to the Grange. Their cultivation of the flower garden and Hareton's primrose-strewn porridge are emblematic of their transformation of the Heights into a domain of feminine values, a haven of tranquillity to which men retire from a workaday world of business and competition, in order to cultivate their gardens, their hobbies and the domestic ideal.
>
> However, at the same time as *Wuthering Heights* traces the emergence of the modern family and its hegemonic fictional form of Domestic realism, other elements of the novel – its disrupted chronology, its dislocated narrative structure, and the persistence of the disturbing power of Catherine and Heathcliff – work together to keep other versions of domestic life before the reader: the domestic space as prison, the family as site of primitive passions, violence, struggle and control.
>
> (from Pykett – see note 16)

Little enough is known directly of Emily Brontë's earliest years; but one crucial fact stands out: her mother died, after a long and painful illness, shortly after Emily's third birthday. I believe that much of what is known of her later life can best be understood in terms of the psychological strategies she developed to deal with the loss of her mother at this crucial point in her development. Likewise, much of what has puzzled readers of *Wuthering Heights* can be understood in terms of struggle, fantasies, and fears associated with the separation-individuation process.

It may seem odd to think of the relationship between Catherine and Heathcliff, which occupies a central position in the novel, as a displaced version of the symbiotic relationship between mother and child. But there is much in the novel to support this view. Emotionally, Heathcliff *is* the world to Catherine, just as the mother *is* the world to the symbiotic child: '"If all else perished, and *he* remained, I should still continue to be; and, if all else remained, and he were annihilated, the Universe would turn to a mighty stranger."' When Catherine discovers that Heathcliff has left, she seeks him as a mother seeks a lost child – or as a lost child seeks its mother: 'calling at intervals, and then listening, and then crying outright. She beat Hareton, or any child, at a good passionate fit of crying'.

(from Wion – see note 12)

I take it that Heathcliff, up to the point at which Cathy rejects him, is in general an admirable character. His account of the Grange adventure, candid, satirical, and self-aware as it is, might itself be enough to enforce this point; and we have in any case on the other side only the self-confessedly biased testimony of Nelly Dean. Even according to Nelly's grudging commentary, Heathcliff as a child is impressively patient and uncomplaining (although Nelly adds 'sullen' out of spite), and the heart-rending cry he raises when old Earnshaw dies is difficult to square with her implication that he felt no gratitude to his benefactor. He bears Hindley's vindictive treatment well, and tries pathetically to keep culturally abreast of Catherine despite it. The novel says quite explicitly that Hindley's systematic degradation of Heathcliff 'was enough to make a fiend of a saint'; and we should not therefore be surprised that what it does, more precisely, is to produce a pitiless capitalist landlord out of an oppressed child. Heathcliff the adult is in one sense an inversion, in another sense an organic outgrowth, of Heathcliff the child. Heathcliff the child was an isolated figure whose freedom from given genealogical ties offered, as I have argued, fresh possibilities of relationship; Heathcliff the adult is the atomic capitalist to whom relational bonds are nothing, whose individualism is now enslaving rather than liberating. The child knew the purely negative freedom of running wild; the adult, as a man vehemently pursuing ends progressively alien to him, knows only the delusory freedom of exploiting others. The point is that such freedom seems the only kind available in this society, once the relationship with Catherine has collapsed; the only mode of self-affirmation left to Heathcliff is that of oppression which, since it involves self-oppression, is no affirmation at all. Heathcliff is a self-tormentor, a man who is in hell because he can avenge himself on the system which has robbed him of his soul only by battling with it on its own hated terms. If as a child he was outside and inside that system simultaneously, wandering on the moors and working on the farm, he lives out of a similar self-division as an adult, trapped in the grinding contradiction between a false social self and the true identity which lies with Catherine. The social self is false not because Heathcliff is only apparently brutal – that he certainly is – but because he is contradictorily related to the authentic selfhood which is his passion for Catherine. He installs himself at the centre of conventional society, but with wholly negative and inimical intent; his social role is a calculated self-contradiction, created first to further, and then fiercely displace, his asocial passion for Catherine.

(from Eagleton – see note 15)

All these interpretations are, I believe, wrong. This is not because each does not illuminate something in *Wuthering Heights*. Each brings something to light, even though it covers something else up in the act of doing so. No doubt my essay too will be open to the charge that it attempts to close off the novel by explaining it, even though that explanation takes the form of an attempted reasonable formulation of its unreason.

My argument is not that criticism is a free-for-all in which one reading is as good as another. No doubt there would be large areas of agreement among competent readers even of this manifestly controversial novel. It is possible to present a reading of *Wuthering Heights* which is demonstrably wrong, not even partially right, though I believe all the readings listed above are in one way or another partially right. They are right because they arise from responses determined by the text. The error lies in the assumption that the meaning is going to be single, unified, and logically coherent. My argument is that the best readings will be the ones which best account for the heterogeneity of the text, its presentation of a definite group of possible meanings which are systematically interconnected, determined by the text, but logically incompatible. The clear and rational expression of such a system of meanings is difficult, perhaps impossible. The fault of premature closure is intrinsic to criticism. The essays on *Wuthering Heights* I have cited seem to me insufficient, not because what they say is demonstrably mistaken, but rather because there is an error in the assumption that there *is* a single secret truth about *Wuthering Heights*. This secret truth would be something formulable as a univocal principle of explanation which would account for everything in the novel. The secret truth about *Wuthering Heights*, rather, is that there is no secret truth which criticism might formulate in this way. No hidden identifiable ordering principle which will account for everything stands at the head of the chain or at the back of the back. Any formulation of such a principle is visibly reductive. It leaves something important still unaccounted for. This is a remnant of opacity which keeps the interpreter dissatisfied, the novel still open, the process of interpretation still able to continue. One form or another of this openness may characterize all works of literature, but this resistance to a single definitive reading takes different forms in different works. In *Wuthering Heights* this special form is the invitation to believe that there is a supernatural transcendent 'cause' for all events, while certain identification of this cause, or even assurance of its existence, is impossible.

Wuthering Heights produces its effect on its reader through the way it is made up of repetitions which permanently resist rational reduction to some satisfying principle of explanation. The reader has the experience, in struggling to understand the novel, that a certain number of the elements which present themselves for explanation can be reduced to order. This act of interpretation always leaves something over, something just at the edge of the circle of theoretical vision which that vision does not encompass. This something left out is clearly a significant detail. There are always in fact a group of such significant details which have been left out of any reduction to order.

(from J. Hillis Miller – see note 19)

Other Brontë writing: links with *Wuthering Heights*

Here we provide a short extract from the opening sections of five novels written by Charlotte and Anne Brontë, along with a very brief indication of the plot of each.

■ From the following introductions, what links can you identify with Emily Brontë's *Wuthering Heights*?

Jane Eyre (1847) by Charlotte Brontë

There was no possibility of taking a walk that day. We had been wandering, indeed, in the leafless shrubbery an hour in the morning; but since dinner (Mrs Reed, when there was no company, dined early) the cold winter wind had brought with it clouds so sombre, and a rain so penetrating, that further outdoor exercise was now out of the question.

I was glad of it; I never liked long walks, especially on chilly afternoons: dreadful to me was the coming home in the raw twilight, with nipped fingers and toes, and a heart saddened by the childings of Bessie, the nurse, and humbled by the consciousness of my physical inferiority to Eliza, John and Georgina Reed.

Jane Eyre is an orphan who is sent to a grim boarding school by unsympathetic relatives. She has an unhappy time, especially when her best friend dies, but eventually becomes a teacher there. She then goes to Thornfield Hall, as the governess of the daughter of Mr Rochester. They fall in love, but the marriage is prevented by the revelation that his mad wife still lives, kept confined to the top floors of the house. Jane runs away, nearly dying on the moors in the process, and is taken in by two sisters who turn out to be her cousins. She nearly marries their brother, but is drawn to return to Thornfield Hall, to find it has burnt down. Rochester's wife died in the fire and he was blinded trying to save her. Jane and Rochester marry and his sight is partially restored.

Shirley (1849) by Charlotte Brontë

Of late years, an abundant shower of curates has fallen upon the north of England: they lie very thick on the hills; every parish has one or more of them; they are young enough to be very active, and ought to be doing a great deal of good. But not of late years are we about to speak; we are going back to the beginning of this century; late years–present years are dusty, sun-burnt, hot, arid; we will evade the noon, forget it in siesta, pass the mid-day in slumber, and dream of dawn.

If you think, from this prelude, that anything like a romance is preparing for you, reader, you were never more mistaken. Do you anticipate sentiment, and poetry, and reverie? Do you expect passion, and stimulus, and melodrama? Calm your expectations; reduce them to a lowly standard. Something real, cool, and solid, lies before you; something unromantic as Monday morning, when all who have work wake with the consciousness that they must rise and betake themselves thereto.

Set in Yorkshire at the time of the Luddite riots, the story tells of a half-Belgian mill owner, Robert Gérard Moore, who introduces labour-saving machinery into his woollen mill, against the wishes of the workers. The workers attempt to destroy the mill and then its owner. In order to solve his financial problems Robert proposes to the wealthy Shirley Keeldar, even though he really loves her quieter cousin Caroline, who also loves him. Shirley rejects him and, when his financial situation improves, he marries Caroline; Shirley marries his brother, Louis.

Villette (1853) by Charlotte Brontë

> My godmother lived in a handsome house in the clean and ancient town of Bretton. Her husband's family had been residents there for generations, and bore, indeed, the name of their birthplace – Bretton of Bretton: whether by coincidence or because some remote ancestor had been a personage of sufficient importance to leave his name to his neighbourhood, I know not.
>
> When I was a girl I went to Bretton about twice a year, and well I liked the visit. The house and its inmates specially suited me. The large peaceful rooms, the well-arranged furniture, the clear wide windows, the balcony outside, looking down on a fine antique street, where Sundays and holidays seemed always to abide – so quiet was its atmosphere, so clean its pavement – these things pleased me well.

A poor, unattractive and lonely English girl, Lucy Snowe, goes as a teacher to a girls' school in Villette (Brussels), where she is successful with the pupils and respected by the headmistress. She seems ready to fall in love with the handsome English school doctor, John Bretton, but instead watches him fall in love first with a flirt, Ginevra Fanshawe, and then, more happily, with Paulina Home. Lucy then gradually falls in love with the less attractive M. Paul Emmanuel, who develops an affection for her in return. When his business takes him to the West Indies he leaves Lucy in charge of her own school. The ending of the novel is left open.

Agnes Grey (1847) by Ann Brontë

> All true histories contain instruction; though in some the treasure may be hard to find, and, when found, so trivial in quantity, that the dry, shrivelled kernel scarcely compensates for the trouble of cracking the nut. Whether this be the case with my history or not, I am hardly competent to judge. I sometimes think it might prove useful to some, and entertaining to others; but the world may judge for itself. Shielded by my own obscurity, and by the lapse of years, and a few fictitious names, I do not fear to venture; and I will candidly lay before the public what I would not disclose to the most intimate friend.
>
> My father was a clergyman of the north of England, who was deservedly respected by all who knew him; and, in his younger days, lived pretty comfortably on the joint income of a small incumbency and a snug little property of his own. My mother, who married him against the wishes of her friends, was a squire's daughter, and a woman of spirit.

Agnes Grey is a a modest and gentle rector's daughter who becomes a governess. She is lonely and treated badly by her employers and the children she teaches, but eventually marries the curate who has previously been kind to her. She is contrasted with the flirtatious and artful Rosalie, Agnes's eldest pupil, who makes a socially ambitious but unsuccessful marriage.

The Tenant of Wildfell Hall (1848) by Ann Brontë

You must go back with me to the autumn of 1827. My father, as you know, was a sort of gentleman farmer in ——shire; and I, by his express desire, succeeded him in the same quiet occupation, not very willingly, for ambition urged me to higher aims, and self-conceit assured me that, in disregarding its voice, I was burying my talent in the earth, and hiding my light under a bushel. My mother had done her utmost to persuade me that I was capable of great achievements; but my father, who thought ambition was the surest road to ruin, and change but another word for destruction, would listen to no scheme for bettering either my own condition, or that of my fellow mortals. He assured me it was all rubbish, and exhorted me, with his dying breath, to continue in the good old way, to follow his steps, and those of his father before him, and let my highest ambition be, to walk honestly through the world, looking neither to the right hand or to the left, and to transmit the paternal acres to my children in, at least, as flourishing a condition as he left them to me.

Gilbert Markham, a young farmer, falls in love with Helen Graham, a beautiful young widow with a small son, who has taken over the tenancy of Wildfell Hall. Her secluded life and the discovery that she meets secretly with her landlord lead to malicious gossip. Gilbert tries to fight her landlord, who is revealed as her brother. She confides her past to Gilbert by giving him her diary, which tells of her miserable marriage to, and escape from, the drunken and corrupt Arthur Huntingdon. She then returns to look after her husband who is seriously ill. When her husband dies, Helen returns to Wildfell Hall and finally marries Gilbert.

Coursework connections

You might want to consider connections between *Wuthering Heights* and other texts for any of the following reasons:

- You are studying *Wuthering Heights* as a coursework text.

- You may want to link work on coursework texts to your study of Wuthering Heights, either through a comparative study or through working on texts where you can draw on what you have learned from studying Wuthering Heights.

- You may simply wish to pursue wider reading to support your study of Wuthering Heights.

Consider the possibilities of the connections we have indicated here, adding further texts and connections yourself. We have elaborated connections with the novels by the Brontë sisters as an example.

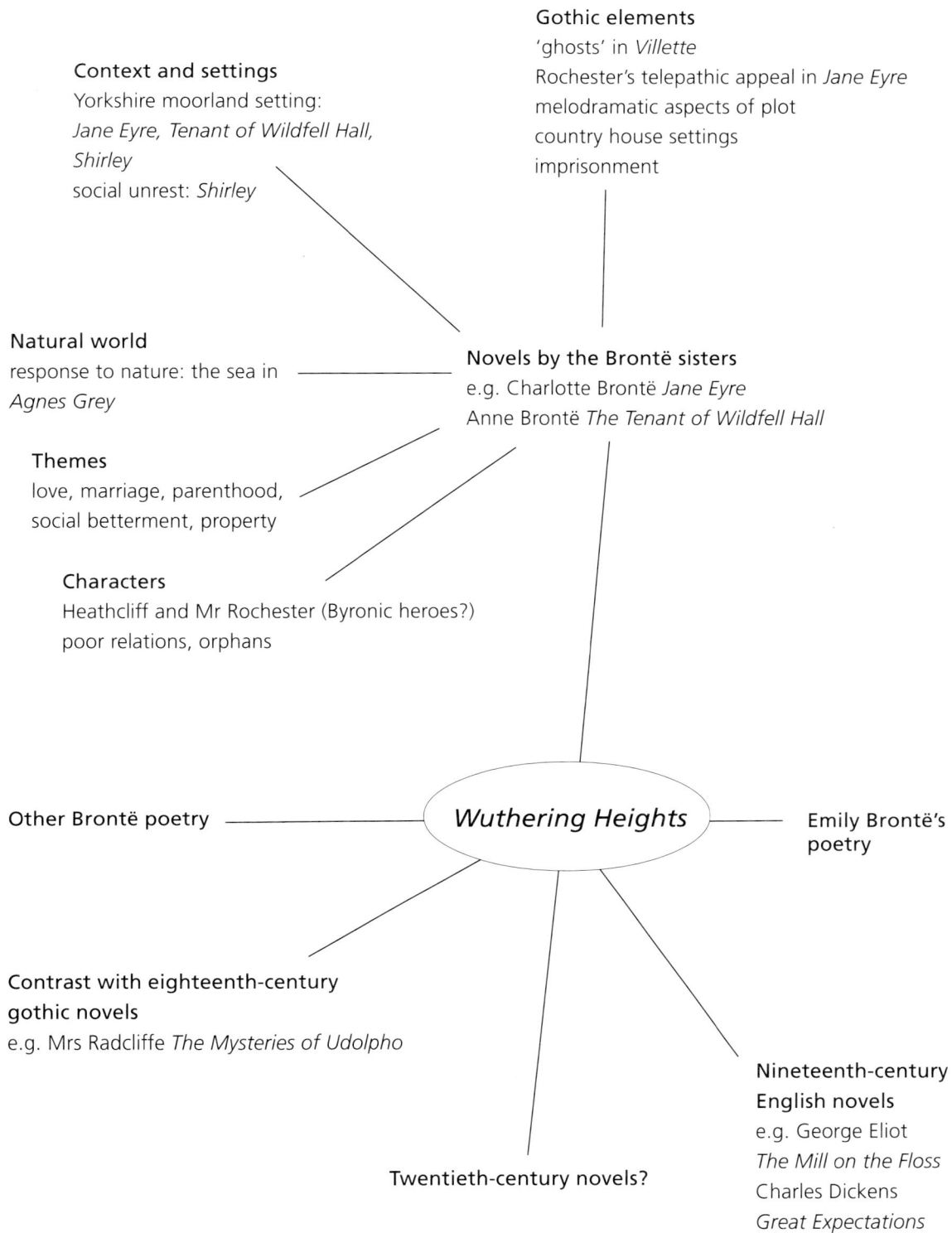

Gothic elements
'ghosts' in *Villette*
Rochester's telepathic appeal in *Jane Eyre*
melodramatic aspects of plot
country house settings
imprisonment

Context and settings
Yorkshire moorland setting:
*Jane Eyre, Tenant of Wildfell Hall,
Shirley*
social unrest: *Shirley*

Natural world
response to nature: the sea in
Agnes Grey

Novels by the Brontë sisters
e.g. Charlotte Brontë *Jane Eyre*
Anne Brontë *The Tenant of Wildfell Hall*

Themes
love, marriage, parenthood,
social betterment, property

Characters
Heathcliff and Mr Rochester (Byronic heroes?)
poor relations, orphans

Other Brontë poetry

Wuthering Heights

**Emily Brontë's
poetry**

**Contrast with eighteenth-century
gothic novels**
e.g. Mrs Radcliffe *The Mysteries of Udolpho*

Twentieth-century novels?

**Nineteenth-century
English novels**
e.g. George Eliot
The Mill on the Floss
Charles Dickens
Great Expectations

Notes

1   Sydney Dobell, *The Life and Letters of Sydney Dobell*, ed. E. Jolly (London: Smith, 1878).

2   See, for example, A. Mary F. Robinson, *Emily Brontë* (Boston: Roberts, 1883).

3   See, for example, Mary Ward's preface to the Haworth edition of *Wuthering Heights* published in 1898.

4   F.R. Leavis and Q.D. Leavis, *Lectures in America* (London: Chatto and Windus, 1969).

5   C.P. Sanger, *The Structure of* Wuthering Heights (London: Hogarth Press, 1926).

6   Lord David Cecil, *Early Victorian Novelists* (London: Constable, 1935).

7   See, for example, Bonamy Dobrée, 'The narrator in *Wuthering Heights*', in Alastair Everitt (ed.) *Wuthering Heights: An Anthology of Criticism* (London: Frank Cass, 1967); or John K. Mathison 'Nelly Dean and the power of *Wuthering Heights*', *Nineteenth Century Fiction*, 11,1956, p. 129.

8   Mark Schorer 'Fiction and the matrix of analogy' *Kenyon Review*, 11, 1949, pp. 539–60.

9   Frank J. Goodridge, 'The circumambient universe', in Thomas A. Vogler (ed.) *Twentieth century Interpretations of* Wuthering Heights (Englewood Cliffs NJ: Prentice-Hall, 1968).

10 Dorothy Van Ghent, *The English Novel: Form and Function* (New York: Holt, 1953)

11 See, for example, Thomas Moser 'What is the matter with Emily Jane? Conflicting impulses in *Wuthering Heights*', *Nineteenth Century Fiction*, 17, 1962, pp. 1–19; or Georges Bataille *La Littérature et le mal* (Paris: Gallimard, 1957).

12 Philip Wion, 'The absent mother in *Wuthering Heights*', in Linda H. Peterson (ed.) *Wuthering Heights* (Basingstoke: Macmillan, 1992); Margaret Homans, 'The name of the mother in *Wuthering Heights*', in Linda H. Peterson (ed.) *Wuthering Heights* (Basingstoke: Macmillan, 1992).

13 Arnold Kettle, *An Introduction to the English Novel* (revised edition, New York: Harper, 1968, originally 1951)

14 Raymond Williams, *The English Novel from Dickens to Lawrence* (Frogmore: Paladin, 1974).

15 Terry Eagleton, *Myths of Power: A Marxist Study of the Brontës* (London: Macmillan,1975).

16 Lyn Pyckett, 'Gender and genre in *Wuthering Heights*: gothic plot and domestic fiction', in Patsy Stoneman (ed.) *Wuthering Heights: Contemporary Critical Essays* (Basingstoke: Macmillan, 1993).

17 Sandra Gilbert, 'Looking oppositely: Emily Brontë's Bible of Hell', in Patsy Stoneman (ed.) *Wuthering Heights: Contemporary Critical Essays* (Basingstoke: Macmillan, 1993).

18 Camille Paglia, 'Sexual personae: the androgyne in literature and art', Yale dissertation, 1974.

19 J. Hillis Miller, '*Wuthering Heights* and the "Uncanny"', in Linda H. Peterson (ed.) *Wuthering Heights* (Basingstoke: Macmillan, 1992).

Bibliography

Brontë, Emily (1992) *Wuthering Heights* Linda H. Peterson (ed.) Basingstoke: Macmillan

Chitham, Edward (1987) *A Life of Emily Brontë*. Oxford: Basil Blackwell

Mengham, Rod (1988) Introduction to Emily Brontë's *Wuthering Heights* (Penguin Critical Studies series). Harmondsworth: Penguin Books

Nestor, Pauline (1995) Introduction to Emily Brontë's *Wuthering Heights* (Penguin Classics edition). Harmondsworth: Penguin Books

Wise, T.J. and Symington, J.A. (eds) (1933) *The Brontës: Their Lives, Friendships and Correspondence*. Oxford: Shakespeare Head

On the Internet there are various web sites relating to *Wuthering Heights* and to the Brontës. These sources are easily accessed by searching for the name 'Brontë' and are well worth skimming through to see if they are of interest to you.